COPING
WITH
FACULTY
STRESS

SURVIVAL SKILLS FOR SCHOLARS

Managing Editor: Mitchell Allen

Survival Skills for Scholars provides you, the professor or advanced graduate student working in a college or university setting, with practical suggestions for making the most of your academic career. These brief, readable guides will help you with skills that you are required to master as a college professor but may have never been taught in graduate school. Using hands-on, jargon-free advice and examples, forms, lists, and suggestions for additional resources, experts on different aspects of academic life give invaluable tips on managing the day-to-day tasks of academia—effectively and efficiently.

Volumes in This Series

SURVIVAL SKILLS FOR SCHOLARS

COPING
WITH
FACULTY
STRESS

WALTER H. GMELCH

SAGE Publications
International Educational and Professional Publisher
Newbury Park London New Delhi

Copyright © 1993 by Sage Publications, Inc.

For information address:

SAGE Publications, Inc.
2455 Teller Road
Newbury Park, California 91320

SAGE Publications Ltd.
6 Bonhill Street
London EC2A 4PU
United Kingdom

SAGE Publications India Pvt. Ltd.
M-32 Market
Greater Kailash I
New Delhi 110 048 India

Printed in the United States of America

Library of Congress Cataloging-in-Publication Data

Gmelch, Walter H.
    Coping with faculty stress / Walter H. Gmelch.
        p.   cm. — (Survival skills for scholars ; v. 5)
    Includes bibliographical references.
    ISBN 0-8039-4969-3. — ISBN 0-8039-4970-7 (pbk.)
    1. College teachers—United States—Job stress. 2. College teaching—United States—Psychological aspects. I. Title. II. Series.
LB2333.3.G58   1993
378.1'2'019—dc20   93-24842

93 94 95 96 10 9 8 7 6 5 4 3 2 1

Sage Production Editor: Judith L. Hunter

Contents

Acknowledgments

The short timeline of Sage's faculty resource guide project and the condensed format of the book posed creative challenges. However, I am forever indebted to Mitch Allen, managing editor, for his vision in creating such a series and his encouragement that it could be done. The work would not have been done without the artistic talent and technological genius of Tracy Schellenberg, who created all the figures, tables, and exercises in camera-ready form. Also, without the support, dedication, and understanding of Lynn Buckley and Patti Komp, I could not have balanced the intrinsic pressure to write this book with the extrinsic responsibility to lead an academic department.

I also want to thank my deans, Bernie Oliver and Sherry Vaughan, my fellow department chairs, my faculty colleagues, Don Reed, Mary Henry, and Don Orlich in particular, and my best friend and colleague Val Miskin, for their encouragement to keep my professional life balanced between my academic and administrative responsibilties. Most importantly, I owe my wife, Paula, and teenage sons, Ben and Tom, my deepest gratitude for their love and understanding since I took the time to write this book at home in the evenings and on weekends. I may not have missed any of my sons' football games this fall but my full attention was not always available when needed.

To the mentors of my professional life as an educator

Allen Brown

Bill Walsh

Ken Erickson

George Gmelch

To the meaning of my life as a father

Ben Gmelch

Tom Gmelch

Preface

The word *stress* is one with which you are familiar. However, for all the attention stress receives, both in publications and in personal experiences, at times, our awareness of what causes us stress remains undiscovered. We know stress exists, but few of us are patient enough to identify its sources to deal with the problem.

A leading authority on stress, Dr. Hans Selye, points out that despite everything that has been written and said about stress and coping behaviors, no single, ready-made solution suits everyone. Since faculty members' thresholds and responses differ, the best a book on faculty stress can hope for is to raise one's consciousness so that pressures of the professorship can be recognized and alleviated before they occur. In the words of an honorable Chinese philosopher:

> Before it move, hold it
> Before it go wrong, mold it
> Drain off water in winter before it freeze
> Before wheat grow, sow them to the breeze
> You can deal with what has not happened, can foresee
> Harmful events and not allow them to be.

This book provides an overview of the most recent ideas and research on faculty stress and presents plans of action for stress reduction. In order to make this book meaningful for faculty, self-assessment instruments, schematic models, and exercises are used throughout the text to assist you in under-standing, internalizing, and applying the key concepts of stress management. To paraphrase another wise Chinese phi-losopher, Confucius: I read and forget, see and remember, and do and understand. It is with this intent that this book is embellished with exercises, figures, and tables.

The information shared in this book is derived from four primary sources. First and foremost, the evidence enabling the composition of this book came from current research and writings on stress, including the author's investigations of the stresses of more than 4,000 faculty members in more than 100 institutions of higher education across the United States. The author is indebted to his coresearchers and colleagues over the past 15 years with whom he has collaborated in the dozens of studies on the stresses of faculty, school administra-tors, and university department chairs—special thanks to Jack Burns, Nick Lovrich, Earl Smith, Boyd Swent, and Kay Wilke.

Second, many of the ideas and passages have emanated from the half dozen books and more than 30 articles the author has written on stress: primarily from such works as *Beyond Stress to Effective Management* (1982), *Coping With Faculty Stress* (1987), and numerous research articles on faculty stress pub-lished in *Research in Higher Education*.

Third, workshop participants who have attended and used the author's materials in more than 500 stress workshops in the past decade throughout the Americas, Europe, Asia, and Africa have provided critical analysis, global perspectives, and insightful comments.

Fourth and finally, the author's personal successes and mis-takes in attempting to cope with both private and public sector stresses as a business executive, professor, researcher, writer, management consultant, and most recently, university administrator. Most authors write about what troubles them the most, and this author is no different. From my burning interest and burned-out attempt to be an author while still maintaining my university administrative responsibilities, this book was created.

1 | Check Your Stress Level

Sometimes I feel I have too heavy a workload, one that I cannot possibly finish in the day . . . or even the academic year.

The words spoken here are not those of a dean squeezed in the middle, a department chair compressed by time pressures, or a secretary frustrated from overload; they came from a tenured full professor looking for a way out.

Yes, time pressure represents one form of stress, just as lethal as feeling helpless within a tenure-track system. No matter what package it comes in, faculty recognize the feeling of stress. It is as much a part of their lives as love, pain, euphoria, and defeat. More than 100,000 books, magazines, and journal articles have been written on stress. Check the campus book stores—their shelves overflow with self-help psychology, exercise, and nutrition books preaching stress control. Virtually every popular psychology, professional, and airline flight magazine prints one article an issue telling their readers how to cope with stress. Now, research journals dedicate entire issues to stress.

Due to multiple uses, references, and definitions, the exact meaning of stress seems ambiguous. Let us begin with the most important definition: your interpretation of stress. Take a minute or two and list in Exercise 1.1 as many one word synonyms for stress as possible. Do not contemplate too long, just write the first words that come to mind.

1

Exercise 1.1
What Is Stress?

List below as many one word synonyms that, to you, mean stress.

1.	11.
2.	12.
3.	13.
4.	14.
5.	15.
6.	16.
7.	17.
8.	18.
9.	19.
10.	20.

From Distress to Eustress

Now, reread your one word definitions. We typically associate stress with terms like *anxiety, frustration, strain*, and the "tension, pressure, pain" we hear from the prolific aspirin commercials. Table 1.1 lists common terms faculty use when asked to define stress. You will notice that they have been subjectively categorized into three columns. The first pertains to the negative stress from the frenzy and fatigue of everyday living. These emanate from pressure situations, uptight feelings, nervous tensions, personal demands, and other unpleasant encounters.

The second column represents words, attitudes, and behaviors which evoke negative feelings at first, but should be considered neutral; that is, if handled properly and put in the right perspective, they could relate to positive experiences as well. Conflict, for example, reminds us of unpleasant encounters with colleagues, but these encounters can also result in positive change, a clearing of the air, new ways of looking at old problems, and creativity. Change represents another good example of something that, in moderation, can be the spice of life, but in excess creates aggravation, frustration, and bewilderment.

The third column contains words considered positive or pleasant. They cause stress, but in a pleasant manner. Consider

Table 1.1 The Three Faces of Stress

DISTRESS (NEGATIVE STRESS)	STRESS (NEUTRAL STRESS)	EUSTRESS (POSITIVE STRESS)
worry	change	tenure
pressure	issue	promotion
anxiety	conflict	challenge
tension	crisis	opportunity
frustration	noise	progress
aggravation	money	acceptance
fear	deadlines	love
annoying	communication	excitement
troublesome	clients	improvement
frantic	criticism	creativity
exasperating	imbalance	friendship
nuisance	discomfort	marriage
trauma	ambiguity	children
confusion	expectations	motivation
strain	schedules	success
bewildered	telephone	achievement
discontent	people	belonging
disappointment	unexpected	stimulation
hate	space	vacation
fatigue		
overload		

your reaction to promotion or tenure. The excitement you feel physiologically creates a stress reaction much as would a cut in pay. Think back to the last frightful experience you had. Let's say you were driving along the road to work and had to swerve off to avoid a head-on collision. How would your body react? A fast heartbeat, increased blood pressure, eyes dilated, rapid breathing, and sweaty palms are common reactions. Now think back to a very pleasurable experience. How about the moment you received tenure? The same bodily reactions probably occurred. So you see, whether stress is positive or negative, your initial physiological reaction is much the same. In essence, stress is a demand on the body, physically or mentally, that exceeds the person's ability to cope.

Figure 1.1. How Do You Spell Stress?

You need to understand the similarity of all stress, whether positive or negative. With our tendency to emphasize the negative effects of stress, we forget to look at the duality of stress. Figure 1.1 characterizes how the Chinese view stress. Each symbol represents a separate character or word the Chinese use to express stress; the first signals *danger* and the other *opportunity*. Like the Chinese representation, we also have words in our language to express both feelings: *distress* for bad or unpleasant events and *eustress* for good or pleasant. Through slurring, the middle English word *distress* came into common English usage as *stress*. *Eustress* came from the Greek prefix of *eu* meaning *good*, like euphoria. You will be reminded throughout this book to change the view of stress as negative—something to rid ourselves of—to one of balance; to recognize and use positive effects of stress to your advantage. Your stress reduction strategy should be to minimize your negative stress factors and maximize the positive ones.

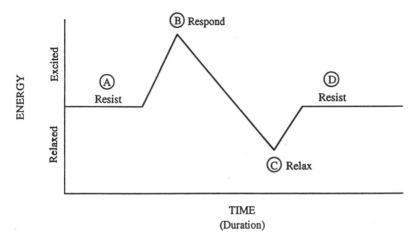

Figure 1.2. TYPE I: Healthy, Short-Term Stress

Types of Tension

Dr. Kenneth Pelletier (1977) points out that stress begins with normal levels of resistance until one encounters a stressor, reacts to it, relaxes after its resolution, and finally returns to normal—until the next stressor attacks. This tension attack can be analyzed in terms of both the time of reaction and the intensity of response.

The Healthy Stress Response

Imagine a typical professor, Sharon Bond, as she reacts to a stressor in terms of time and intensity as plotted in Figure 1.2; the time of her stress reaction along the horizontal *duration* axis against the intensity of her stress reaction up the vertical *energy* axis. Much as Pelletier (1977) explains, Sharon begins with a normal level of resistance or energy (point A), until a stressor attacks, prompting her reaction (point B). After Sharon resolves the stressor, a period of relaxation follows (point C), and she finally returns to a normal state of resistance (point D).

This figure illustrates what doctors consider a short-term, healthy response to stress; it is one in which faculty can resolve the problem and return to a steady state of resistance for a period before the next challenge arises. Physiological response to a threat or an opportunity follows this same pattern. We perceive what threatens us, decide what action needs to be taken, take action, breathe a sigh of relief once resolved, and finally return to normal tasks at hand. The key to a short-term, healthy reaction rests in:

1. identifying the stressor,
2. applying an action to resolve it, and
3. taking the time to bring back a calm state for restoration of energy before taking on the next challenge.

The Hazardous Stress Response

In contrast, Figure 1.3 depicts the hazardous, long-term stress that cannot be quickly resolved, has no clear cause or method of resolution, and leaves no time to return to a steady state of relaxation.

Let us look at a typical day in Professor Bond's life. She drives to her office through push-and-shove, lane-changing traffic from 7 a.m. to 8 a.m. to find her desk cluttered with yesterday's unfinished tasks and the floor stacked with ungraded papers and unfinished manuscripts. Before work can be organized into manageable tasks, a well-wishing colleague drops in for a morning chat, followed by a rapid succession of unexpected telephone calls. The day's activities never seem to get organized. Even without interruptions from the telephone, office staff, or drop-in visitors, Sharon switches from one knotty task to another without having the benefit of even a brief sigh of relief.

The fragmented, unproductive morning forces the now harried Sharon to cancel her monthly luncheon with her best friend. She guiltily decides to substitute a healthy lunch with another cup of coffee at her desk and proceeds to spill it over

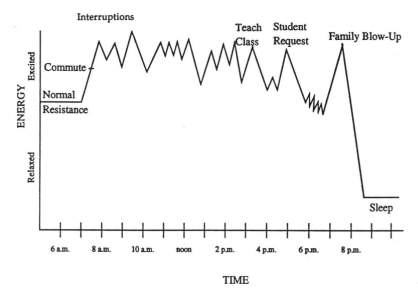

Figure 1.3. TYPE II: Hazardous, Long-Term Stress

the exams she is to administer in her 3 o'clock class. As the exams have to be retyped, she feels even more hurried and behind. At 2 p.m. she blows up at a student's request to miss today's class. Her day continues with interruptions, confrontations, and unfulfilled expectations. At 4 p.m., after class, she calls home to announce her projected late arrival. Finally, our frustrated, downtrodden professor arrives home at 8 p.m. to find her family disappointed and distant. Feeling boxed in, Sharon reminds them that she tries her best to provide for them and the least they could do is understand and empathize with the tremendous pressures she has been under at the college. She closes the family conversation with a curt "good-night" and exits to her "home office."

The Harmonic Stress Response

Now we will look at how Sharon could approach her day by combining the healthy stress pattern portrayed in Figure 1.2

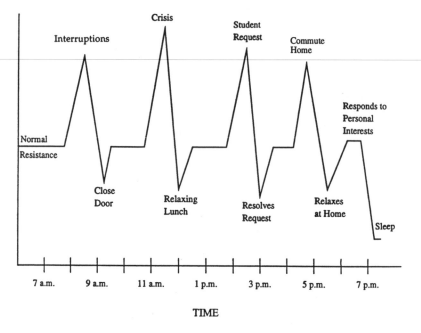

Figure 1.4. TYPE III: Harmonic Stress

with the potentially hazardous and chronic stress pattern in Figure 1.3. Sharon, in Figure 1.4, provides a harmonic approach to what was once a disastrous day. Her day begins much the same, with an hour commute, though she does not switch lanes to reduce seconds, but chooses one lane, and rides it all the way to work while listening to the local classical music station.

Upon arriving at her office she immediately begins organizing her cluttered desk. At 8:30 a.m. her desk looks very different; only her day's "to do" list and appointment calendar are visible. Although Sharon receives a telephone call and a drop-in colleague within the next few minutes, she decides to complete some tasks instead of dealing with the two interruptions. She asks the office staff to hold all calls, she shuts her door, and then calmly sets out to accomplish a few of the essentials on her list. At 11:00 a.m. she frees herself up again, returns telephone calls, and responds to student requests. She meets the sudden student crisis with a calm and rational process, searching for alternative solutions and coming up with one that will allow the student to make up the class.

Feeling good about her morning accomplishments, she meets her colleague at the faculty club for lunch, takes an extra 15 minutes to return to the office via a more scenic route and takes time to smell the proverbial roses. Sharon starts the afternoon with a sense of calmness, tackling the important tasks first, then beginning the more routine and mundane. She prepares for her class and enters the classroom at 3 p.m., prepared and ready with a passion for her subject matter. After class she takes time to meet with some students, then begins her commute at 5 p.m. for a relaxing time at home with her family.

Plot Your Tension

Now is your chance to graphically portray a typical day in your professorial life. Use Figure 1.5 to plot your day in terms of stressors, responses, and periods of relaxation. Use one day this week as a starting point. Take a check of your energy state every hour, on the hour, and plot where you have been and where you are currently. This provides you with your first checkup on the type of tension you experience. Was it hazardous or harmonic? Chapter 2 will help you begin the road to reduced stress by taking the tension points you have identified in Figure 1.5 and searching for realistic solutions.

Stress and Performance: The Positive Value of Stress

How do you perform under pressure? Why do some faculty members cope quite well while others collapse? What is the relationship between stress and your faculty performance? The answers to these questions fill volumes of books and journals in the library.

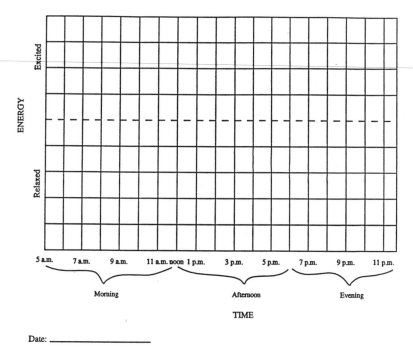

Figure 1.5. Plot Your Stress

Blackburn (1979) found that the discrepancy between productive and nonproductive faculty increases over time. That is, productive faculty maintain their high level and less productive faculty become even more so. His research leads to several truths about academic careers that impact faculty members' productivity and creativity.

1. Faculty productivity is predictable, depending on the age they started becoming productive for the institution and when they received their advanced degree.
2. Faculty productivity is determined to a high degree by the institution.
3. Faculty productivity is influenced by organizational factors like leadership, support, control of the environment, and selection of colleagues.

4. Faculty productivity is influenced by time structure, which affects performance.
5. Faculty tasks and interests vary during the academic career.
6. Age is not a predictor of faculty members' productivity because the level of productivity remains more or less stable during the academic career.
7. Having a mentor and the existence of a network are important factors during the first years of an academic career.
8. Faculty productivity is stifled by uncertainty and risk taking, but competition produces better results than complacency.
9. Faculty are productive principally because of intrinsic rewards. (Blackburn, 1979, pp. 25-26)

From those observations it is easy to infer the relationship between stress and faculty productivity. While the effects of stress on performance eludes precise measurement, the association can be portrayed in an inverted U-shaped curve. As you can see from the diagram in Figure 1.6, stress ranges from low to high along the horizontal axis, while performance ranges from low to high on the vertical axis. The association between stress and performance results in three zones of faculty productivity: under, optimum, and over (Gmelch, 1983). The first zone exemplifies what happens when faculty are underchallenged or understimulated and productivity is low. In effect, they *rust-out* from teaching the same classes for the past decade and suffer from boredom, fatigue, and dissatisfaction with their profession. At the other extreme are faculty who have been going too hard for too long and *burn-out*. They exhibit ambitious, aggressive, and impatient characteristics like those of Type A described in Chapter 3. These are not bad traits in themselves, but these faculty members have not yet learned their limitations and burn themselves out. Burnout affects the whole person, including intellectual, mental, emotional, social, and physical performances (Tubesing & Tubesing, 1982).

However, stress in itself and in the proper amounts is not bad. It can be compared to your body temperature; you must

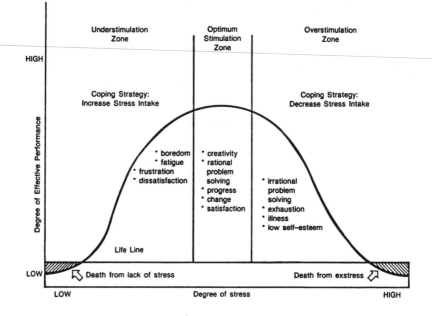

Figure 1.6. Stress and Performance
SOURCE: Adapted from *Beyond Stress to Effective Management*, Gmelch, 1982, p. 29.
Printed with permission.

have it to exist, but it must remain at the proper level. The prescription is logical: increase your stress intake (take on more responsibility and new assignments) when you are understimulated and decrease stress intake (reduce the unnecessary overload) when overstimulated. As we found from our study of professors across the country, when they experience moderate stress, they function at peak performance, whether they are teaching, providing service, or engaging in scholarship (Wilke, Gmelch, & Lovrich, 1985).

Coping With Stress Holistically

The research on coping leads to one final conclusion: Those who cope best do not rely primarily on one coping technique but develop a repertoire of techniques to counteract different stressors in different situations. When we asked over 2,000 academics the following question, "Recognizing that your job is a demanding one, what ways have you found useful in handling the pressures of your job?" The majority gave more than one response. In all, over 3,226 coping responses were identified. Content analysis of these responses revealed seven coping categories (Gmelch, 1988). Review the following categories to see if you have a robust repertoire which includes coping techniques in each area.

- *Social Support* such as having lunch with colleagues, talking with a trusted friend, sharing frustrations with your spouse, consulting with other faculty, and talking to "yourself" a lot.
- *Physical Activities* including individual sports such as jogging, swimming, walking, hiking, golf, and skiing as well as team sports like tennis, racquetball, and basketball.
- *Intellectual Stimulation* from attending professional conferences, keeping up with the literature in your field, writing manuscripts, teaching, attending cultural events, and reading broadly.
- *Entertainment* from going to a movie, going out to dinner, watching television, taking a mini-vacation, and attending a concert or community event.
- *Personal Interest* techniques such as playing a musical instrument, gardening, gourmet cooking, working on crafts, and other personal hobbies unrelated to work.
- *Self-Management* techniques such as time management, dealing with conflict creatively, being assertive, effective committee work, setting goals, and delegation.
- *Supportive Attitudes* such as being optimistic, keeping a positive outlook, having private sayings, reciting religious scriptures, and developing personal philosophies.

While neither a single category nor one of the responses taken separately presents the answer for coping, taken collectively faculty can use these seven categories as a coping taxonomy from which to develop a balance and holistic coping profile. Much like weight loss, if you were to exercise more, but eat more too, the result may not be as beneficial as exercising more while cutting back on food consumption at the same time. In much the same way, effective coping occurs when you build a repertoire of techniques balanced in the areas of social support, physical activity, intellectual stimulation, entertainment, self-management, personal interest, and supportive attitudes. Your goal should be to add techniques to your present repertoire of coping responses.

Stress can be the spice of your life, if you handle it right!

2 | Identify Your Stress Traps

Education is to professors as water is to goldfish.
They swim in it, but never think to study it.
Attributed to John W. Gardner

This statement reflects the relative dearth of studies in which college and university professors are the focus. While academicians devote much time and energy to the study of other professions, they rarely turn that scrutiny on themselves. Few have ventured to study the professoriate, and when exploring its dimensions the discourse most often remains at the philosophical and esoteric levels.

Earlier studies reveal that professors are among those professionals who are most satisfied with their jobs, and report fewer health problems. However, recent studies of academics around the word reveal dissatisfaction with work environments, disillusionment with career progress, and consequences of stress emanating from various aspects of their professional roles. The decade of the 1980s has produced a generation of professors attempting to cope with unexpectedly high levels of change and stress. In American universities and colleges more than half the faculty actively seek positions in other institutions, and nearly one-third consider changing careers (Bowen & Schuster, 1986).

In light of this evidence, faculty stress may be of increasing importance to your morale and productivity. This chapter focuses on ways you can identify your stressors. First, the faculty stress cycle introduces you to a four stage model which

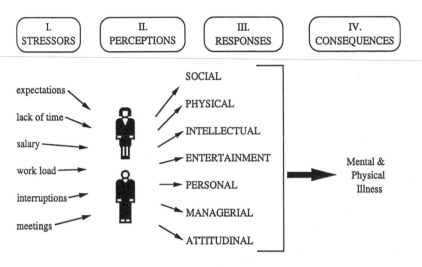

Figure 2.1. The Stress Cycle

provides a framework for managing your stress. Second, you will explore what bothers you, the stressors as the first stage of your stress cycle. Finally, you will identify techniques to master the stresses in your profession.

The Faculty Stress Cycle

As a faculty member, rather than avoiding stress, you need to control it and use it to your advantage. The four stage Faculty Stress Cycle portrayed in Figure 2.1 provides a broad perspective and clear understanding of stress and introduces a framework for action. The process begins with Stage 1, *stressors*, a set of specific demands. Excessive self-expectations, meetings, interruptions, and confrontations represent some common faculty stressors. How much stress is produced by these stressors depends on Stage 2, your *perception* of these demands. If you do not have the physical or mental resources to meet the demand, you perceive the demand as a stress trap.

Stress created by this discrepancy between demand and personal resources results in a specific stress *response*, Stage 3. The fourth and final stage, *consequences*, reflects the intensity and long-range negative effects of stress. This book focuses on all four stages of the stress cycle for faculty: identify your stress traps, Stage 1; investigate whether your own personality is killing you, Stage 2; broaden your repertoire of effective coping responses, Stage 3; and convert the possible negative consequences to peak performance by balancing your life, Stage 4. If the stressors can be identified, negative perceptions turned into positive ones, and a variety of responses used in flexible and creative ways, then the consequences will produce a productive professor.

Faculty Stress Traps

Begin to control your four stage stress cycle by examining the demands of your current situation. What are your stress traps as a faculty member? Meetings, interruptions, insufficient time to keep current, conflicts with colleagues, and pressures to publish all represent potential stressors. While a single telephone interruption may not cause a great deal of difficulty, combining the interruption with an unexpected request from your department chair, an irate student, or a backlog of paperwork, and you're likely to find yourself having a stress attack.

Synergistic and Single Event Stress Attacks

The key to stress reduction rests with identifying your stress traps. Within a few minutes one telephone interruption combined with another and another on top of an already overloaded day creates more tension than if each stressor had attacked and been dealt with separately. In essence, the interaction of stressors becomes synergistic; that is, a minor irritant combined with several others becomes explosive, whereas each single attack alone may cause little or no stress. This results in what we call synergistic stress—the cumulative action of separate stressors having total effect greater than the sum of their individual effects.

In contrast to synergistic stress, a single event stressor may, by itself, be dramatic enough to cause a major stress reaction. Receiving an unjustified annual review, having a manuscript rejected, or getting poor student evaluations all represent situations significant enough to create a severe stress reaction.

A necessary precursor to managing stress, whether synergetic or single event, is to recognize stress as a problem and do something about it. The stress log in Exercise 2.1 represents the most helpful tool to identify what troubles you as a professor. The log is based on the assumption that we can mentally perceive what is bothering us without relying solely on physiological devices such as biofeedback machines.

Specific instructions on how to use your stress log are outlined below. After reviewing them, start your log this week and continue recording stressors for at least a two-week period.

Instructions: Before leaving your office each day, record the following:

Column 1: Write the single most stressful event that occurred during the day (e.g., conflict with a colleague).

Column 2: Write the most stressful series of related events that occurred during the day (e.g., frequent telephone interruptions).

Column 3: Indicate your numerical assessment of how the day went. Do not contemplate too long but give your first impression from "1" (not very stressful) to "10" (very stressful).

After you have kept a log for a week, read over your list of stressors and add at the bottom of the log any other stressful situations that usually occur but for some reason did not occur during this particular week. Then, review your log and see if certain ones reappeared several times. If so, is there a pattern to their recurrence? Reflect on your scores in Column 3. What kind of week did you have?

Exercise 2.1
Stress Log

Stress can come from a single dramatic incident (Single Event Stress), or from a cumulation of less dramatic related incidents (Synergetic Stress).

For one week, at the end of each working day, describe:

1. The most stressful single incident that occurred on your job (confronting a staff member, etc.).
2. The most stressful series of related incidents that occurred on your job (frequent telephone interruptions, etc.).
3. How your day went. Indicate from "1" (not very stressful) to "10" (very stressful) the approximate level of your stress for each day.

	(1) Single Incident	(2) Series of Related Incidents	(3) Daily Stress Level
Monday Date:			
Tuesday Date:			
Wednesday Date:			
Thursday Date:			
Friday Date:			

Please indicate below other stressful incidents which usually occur, but did not during this particular week.

1.

2.

Follow these first week reflections with a second week stress log. Some new troublesome stressors may surface from the second week's log. You may also begin to see possible patterns or cycles like those identified in Chapter 1. Did you find Tuesdays bogged down with too many inefficient meetings?

Are days with your heaviest teaching load the most stressful, or most enjoyable? If you find your work repetitive and predictable, your stress attacks will follow the same pattern, not only daily and weekly, but throughout the semester and academic year.

Not all of your stress traps may be identified from a two-week stress log. Exercise 2.2 identifies 45 common causes of faculty stress. These items were developed from a series of national and institutional studies. In order to ensure that all potentially relevant facets of faculty related stress were identified, the items on the Faculty Stress Index were compiled from several sources. First, dozens of faculty members kept stress logs for a period of two weeks in order to indicate on a daily basis the most stressful single event and most stressful series of events. Second, a survey of faculty responsibilities added additional items. Third, other instruments developed to assess stress in academe were investigated. Finally, a national study of more than 1,200 college and university faculty members was conducted in 100 institutions of higher education (Gmelch, Lovrich, & Wilke, 1984). The compilation of items from all these sources resulted in the 45 item Faculty Stress Index (FSI).

Now you probably know more than you needed to know about the FSI, but true academics always want to know the source of information to check for validity and reliability, especially if they are about to take it themselves. Now, go ahead and complete Exercise 2.2 to search for the sources of your stress. Read through the items and rate them from "1" (rarely or never stressful) to "5" (frequently stressful).

After you have rated each item, identify your five most bothersome stressors (Exercise 2.2, Part B). As a reference point, the most serious stressors from the 1,200 faculty members in the national study are listed in Table 2.1. Overall, faculty reported that 60% of the total stress in their lives came from their work.

Faculty representing all disciplines were included in this study and when faculty stressors were compared within disciplinary groupings, far more similarities than differences

Exercise 2.2
Faculty Stress Index

The following work-related situations have been identified as potential sources of stress. It is possible that some of these situations cause more pressure than others. Indicate to what extent each is a source of pressure by circling the appropriate response.

	Not Applicable	Slight Pressure	Moderate Pressure	Excessive Pressure	
1. Participating in the work of departmental or university committees	NA	1	2	3	4	5
2. Participating in work-related activities outside regular working hours	NA	1	2	3	4	5
3. Meeting social obligations (clubs, parties, volunteer work) expected of me because of my position	NA	1	2	3	4	5
4. Complying with departmental and university rules and regulations	NA	1	2	3	4	5
5. Having inadequate facilities (office, library, laboratories, classrooms)	NA	1	2	3	4	5
6. Evaluating the performance of students	NA	1	2	3	4	5
7. Making presentations at professional conferences and meetings	NA	1	2	3	4	5
8. Imposing excessively high self-expectations	NA	1	2	3	4	5
9. Receiving inadequate university recognition for community services	NA	1	2	3	4	5
10. Having students evaluate my teaching performance	NA	1	2	3	4	5
11. Resolving differences with fellow faculty members	NA	1	2	3	4	5
12. Having insufficient time to keep abreast of current developments in my field	NA	1	2	3	4	5
13. Having insufficient authority to perform my responsibilities	NA	1	2	3	4	5
14. Believing that the progress in my career is not what it should or could be	NA	1	2	3	4	5
15. Assignment of duties that take me away from my office	NA	1	2	3	4	5

	Not Applicable	Slight Pressure	Moderate Pressure	Excessive Pressure	
16. Being interrupted frequently by telephone calls and drop-in visitors	NA	1	2	3	4	5
17. Securing financial support for my research	NA	1	2	3	4	5
18. Frequently being requested to provide community services	NA	1	2	3	4	5
19. Teaching/advising inadequately prepared students	NA	1	2	3	4	5
20. Preparing a manuscript for publication	NA	1	2	3	4	5
21. Being unclear as to the scope and responsibilities of my job	NA	1	2	3	4	5
22. Having insufficient reward for institutional/ departmental service	NA	1	2	3	4	5
23. Having inadequate time for teaching preparation	NA	1	2	3	4	5
24. Feeling pressure to compete with my colleagues	NA	1	2	3	4	5
25. Having repetitious teaching and job assignments	NA	1	2	3	4	5
26. Writing letters and memos, and responding to other paper work	NA	1	2	3	4	5
27. Resolving differences with students	NA	1	2	3	4	5
28. Having insufficient time for performing the service function	NA	1	2	3	4	5
29. Feeling that I have too heavy a work load, one that I cannot possibly finish during the normal work day	NA	1	2	3	4	5
30. Attending meetings which take up too much time	NA	1	2	3	4	5
31. Dealing with program changes or reduced enrollment impact my job	NA	1	2	3	4	5
32. Receiving insufficient recognition for teaching performance	NA	1	2	3	4	5
33. Making class presentations	NA	1	2	3	4	5
34. Trying to influence my chair's actions and decisions which affect me	NA	1	2	3	4	5
35. Not having clear criteria for evaluating service activities	NA	1	2	3	4	5

	Not Applicable	Slight Pressure		Moderate Pressure		Excessive Pressure
36. Resolving differences with my chair	NA	1	2	3	4	5
37. Lacking congruency in institutional, departmental, and personal goals	NA	1	2	3	4	5
38. Having to teach subject matter for which I am not sufficiently prepared	NA	1	2	3	4	5
39. Receiving insufficient institutional recognition for research performance	NA	1	2	3	4	5
40. Lacking personal impact on departmental/ institutional decision making	NA	1	2	3	4	5
41. Not knowing how my chair evaluates my performance	NA	1	2	3	4	5
42. Receiving inadequate salary to meet financial needs	NA	1	2	3	4	5
43. Not having clear criteria for evaluation of research and publication activities	NA	1	2	3	4	5
44. Having job demands which interfere with other personal activities (recreation, family, and other interests)	NA	1	2	3	4	5
45. Being drawn into conflict between colleagues	NA	1	2	3	4	5

Please add other sources of work-related stress:

46.	1	2	3	4	5
47.	1	2	3	4	5
48. Assess the level of stress you experience in your job	1	2	3	4	5
49. Assess the level of stress you experience in your daily life	1	2	3	4	5

From the items on the previous pages, list the top 5 most bothersome situations you encounter.

1. _____

2. _____

3. _____

4. _____

5. _____

Table 2.1 Ten Most Troublesome Stress Traps for Professors

1. Imposing excessively high self-expectations
2. Securing financial support for scholarship
3. Having insufficient time to keep abreast with developments in field
4. Receiving insufficient salary
5. Striving to publish one's scholarship
6. Having too heavy a workload
7. Job demands interfering with personal activities
8. Feeling progress in career is not what it could be
9. Receiving interruptions from telephone and drop-in visitors
10. Attending too many meetings

existed in the way faculty across academia viewed stress. Also, a comparison of sources and patterns of occupational stress reported by Israeli faculty (Keinan & Perlberg, 1987) to the American counterparts (Gmelch, Lovrich, & Wilke, 1984) revealed a similar ranking of the major sources of stress. The problem of stress in academic settings is generic, common to many disciplines and cultures rather than specific to a few.

However, a study of 1,807 academics in a single comprehensive higher education institution found sources of stress varied across seven classifications of faculty and administration, from resident instructional faculty to department chairs. The following results and stress patterns might be of interest to you and your colleagues across campus.

Resident Instructional Faculty. With the exception of their number-one stressor (self-expectations), instructional faculty identified lack of resources as a common theme in their list of top stressors. For example, the next four highest stressors were "securing financial support," "having insufficient time to keep abreast of current developments in my field," "receiving inadequate salary," and "too heavy a workload."

Department Chairs. Chairs were seen as trapped between the pressures and demands of performing not only as a faculty member, but also as an administrator. Those pressures unique to department chairs were "establishing compatibility among institutional, departmental, and personal goals," "completing paperwork on time," "attending meetings," and "dealing with the university rules and regulations," At the same time they suffered from such common faculty stressors as "insufficient time to keep abreast of developments in my discipline," "too heavy a workload," and "securing financial support for my research." Thus they find themselves in a paradoxical situation of sitting in a swivel chair turning to pressures both as a faculty member and as an administrator (see Gmelch, 1992).

Academic Administrators. Not surprisingly, three of the top stressors for academic administrators addressed the issue of institutional service: "being engaged in service activities" (ranked first), "making presentations," and "having insufficient time for service activities." The second theme that characterized academic administrators related to having responsibility for individuals, for example, "supervising and coordinating the tasks of many people" and "having to make decisions that affect the lives of others."

Librarians. The nature of librarian stress combines both administrator and faculty pressures: limited time and resources. However, the specific stressors that bother them are somewhat different. In regard to time, the most bothersome areas were "too heavy a workload," "attending meetings," "participating in work-related activities outside regular working hours," "insufficient time to keep abreast of developments in my field," and "job demands interfering with personal time." These events represented five of the top seven stressors; the remaining two dealt with "inadequate facilities" and "inadequate salary."

Student Services. Stress for student services administrators emanated from a variety of sources, with no single theme predominant. For example, two of the top stressors related to time, while "inadequate salary" represented the top stressor.

Cooperative Extension. Consistent with administrative groups, cooperative extension faculty identified time as their major source of stress. The pressures of time were further compounded by their inability to control "frequent interruptions" and "paperwork."

Nonacademic Administrators. Probably the most diverse set of stressors were experienced by nonacademic administrators who suffered from multiple sources of stress such as "excessively high self-expectations," "too heavy a workload," "insufficient time to keep current," "trying to gain financial support for programs," and "frequent interruptions" (Gmelch & Wilke, 1991, pp. 30-31).

Factors of Faculty Stress

From all these stressors, are there common themes or clusters of stressors that plague faculty? Factor analysis of the 45 items indicates the presence of five distinct clusters, that in combination, account for most of the faculty stress (Gmelch, Wilke, & Lovrich, 1986). As you think about areas in the academy that trouble you, reflect on these five major sources of frustration.

❶ *Reward and recognition.* The majority of stress emanates from faculty rewards and recognition: inadequate rewards, insufficient recognition, and unclear expectations in all three areas of faculty responsibility—teaching, research, and service.

❷ *Time constraints.* This factor reflects faculty members' feelings of insufficient time to keep abreast of current developments, inadequate time for class preparation, interruptions from telephones and drop-in visitors, writing memos and letters, attending meetings, too heavy a workload, and job demands interfering with personal activities. Many of these problems are similar to those experienced by department chairs.

❸ *Departmental influence.* The third area deals with attempts to influence chairs' decisions, resolving differences with chairs, understanding how chairs evaluate faculty performance, and the overall lack of impact on departmental and institutional decision making.

❹ *Professional identity.* It is not surprising that the professional identity factor emerges since faculty reputation is built on scholarship: publications, presentations to conferences, grants, and research. Add to this the stressor of imposing excessively high self-expectations (the highest stressor for faculty) and this represents the foundation of faculty stress.

❺ *Student interaction.* The final factor relates to the interaction between students and colleagues. Faculty members find themselves in conflict with students over evaluation, advising and teaching.

Upon further analysis, this study found that as faculty received tenure and moved to higher academic ranks of associate and full professor, not all areas of faculty stress declined. However, only the stress from *time constraints* and *professional identity* declined with age and experience. Faculty gender and marital status also varied significantly with the same two of the five factors. Married women professors experienced more stress from time constraints and personal identity. Overall, the findings suggest that higher stress levels in regard to some stress factors are associated with lower rank and untenured status as well gender, marital status, age, and experience.

This research leads to some truisms about academic stress that you should consider.

1. Faculty stress is somewhat predictable, depending on age, gender, and marital status.
2. Faculty stress is influenced by tenure and rank.
3. Faculty stress is determined to a high degree by the institutional reward structure.
4. Faculty stress is influenced by time constraints impeding the way to productivity.
5. Faculty stress is influenced by the perception of one's own expectations.
6. Faculty stress is universal across all academic disciplines.

Coping Strategies

Before applying the research findings to your coping strategies, current implications from the research on coping are important to highlight. The literature is significant in volume and diverse in attention. Coping research addresses popular and academic concerns as well as conceptualized, theoretical, and empirical investigations. Researchers from the disciplines of medicine, political science, psychiatry, clinical psychology, behavior science, and education have undertaken studies to understand the phenomenon of stress and coping responses. The following propositions on coping are asserted as a basis for this next section and for this book in general:

1. The individual is the most important variable; no single coping technique is effective for all faculty in all institutions.
2. Faculty cannot change the world around them, but they can change how they relate to it.
3. Coping techniques must be sensitive to cultural, gender, social, psychological, and environmental differences in individuals and institutions.
4. Faculty who cope best develop a repertoire of techniques to counteract different stressors in different situations.
5. A faculty member's repertoire of techniques should represent a holistic approach to coping, such as exercise, social support, sound dietary practices, self-management skills, personal hobbies, and supportive attitudes.

The following sections address both the individual and institutional strategies you may wish to employ to defuse your stress traps.

Individual Strategies: The Faculty Action Plan

How can you cope with your individual stress traps? Is there a definitive strategy which, if used, can help you systematically address the stresses in higher education? Adams

(1980) suggests a three-level approach to stress management: (a) remove or avoid unnecessary stressors; (b) cope effectively with necessary stressors; and (c) build health to buffer long-term effects of stress. The coping strategy posited in this book suggests that you divide your stress traps into two categories: (a) those internally controlled by you, and (b) those externally beyond your control. Those within your control should be attacked at the cause level by self-management techniques. Those beyond your control should be cushioned at the symptom level with stress absorbers such as relaxation, nutrition, exercise, and coping attitudes (Gmelch, 1982).

The majority of top faculty stress traps deal with time and resource constraints—insufficient time to keep abreast of developments in your field, drop-in visitors, as well as insufficient salaries and the difficulties in securing financial support for your research. Clearly, some of these stressors are more within your control than others. Most faculty would agree that while they could become better managers of their time, it is more difficult to directly impact salaries in such trying economic tmes. Overall, much of the stress faculty experience might be alleviated with a reappraisal of individual capabilities and limitations. Faculty must learn to manage the stress traps within their control.

The Faculty Action Plan in Exercise 2.3 will help you successfully reduce menacing stressors. The purpose of the plan is to systematically dissect and redirect your stress. In doing so you can analyze the causes of each stressor, examine potential solutions, and finally take correction actions. Specifically, take the following steps to complete your Faculty Action Plan.

❶ *Identify a stress trap to resolve.* As a beginning, the Faculty Stress Index gives you a list of potential problems to pursue. You listed the top five most bothersome stress traps from this index in Exercise 2.2 so why not start here? For example, Figure 2.2 identifies "too heavy a workload" as a common faculty stressor.

❷ *Search for the causes of the stressful event.* Failure to resolve stress stems from one basic fact: The cause has not been discovered. Unlike simple problems, stressors sometimes result from a multitude of causes. What are causes of a "heavy workload?" Some of the culprits outlined in Figure 2.2 include "unrealistic appraisal of time," "inability to say no," and "inability to distinguish between high and low priorities."

❸ *Generate a set of possible solutions to remedy the causes.* This step identifies alternatives that will alleviate the causes you have previously outlined. You will need to identify solutions for each cause. For example, to attack the cause of "unrealistic appraisal of time" a logical solution would be to first keep a personal time log to audit how and where you presently spend your time.

❹ *Specify a plan to alleviate a cause.* Now you are ready to take action. Review your set of solutions and select one solution as a plan that suits you best. What impact do you feel your plan will have on reducing or alleviating your stress? Typically, plans of action can produce any one of five actions: (a) *Interim,* which keeps you going while you search for a long-term solution; (b) *Adaptive,* when you find out that the causes are unresolvable or unremovable; (c) *Corrective,* which eliminates the cause of the stress; (d) *Preventive,* which removes the possible cause of the stressor, or the probability of it occurring before it attacks; and (e) *Contingency,* which provides stand-by actions to offset or minimize the effects of a serious stress attack.

❺ *Develop a timetable to implement the plan.* Your next task is to integrate your plan into your everyday professional style. You will need to restate *what* you will be doing (e.g., prioritizing tasks each day into high payoff and low payoff activities); *where* (e.g., in your office); and *how often* and *when* (e.g., every day as soon as you arrive on campus).

❻ *Set a date and method to follow-up and evaluate the effectiveness of the plan.* Any plan should contain steps to review and assess your progress, followed by modification of the action if it produced unwanted results. This is the purpose of steps 6 and 7.

❼ *Investigate potential problems or unintended consequences the plan may have created.* Any change will cause some stress. Because your plan has most likely changed your behavior, assess what additional stress and strain you may have caused due to your new plan of action. If these unintended consequences should be alleviated, make modifications in your plan to reduce these unwanted side effects.

Exercise 2.3
Faculty Action Plan

I. Most Bothersome Stress Event: _____

II. CAUSES	III. SOLUTIONS	IV. SPECIFIC ACTION PLAN
1.	1.	a) The plan is to:
2.	2.	
3.	3.	
4.	4.	
5.	5.	

V. STEPS FOR IMPLEMENTATION	
1. Activity:	3. How often:
2. Where:	4. When:

VI. FOLLOW-UP EVALUATION	
1.	3.
2.	4.

VII. NEGATIVE UNINTENDED CONSEQUENCES	
1.	3.
2.	4.

SOURCE: © Walter H. Gmelch, *Beyond Stress to Effective Management*, The Wiley Press, 1982.

Although the Faculty Action Plan may seem too mechanical and systematic, its logic is exactly what makes it work. For guidance, Figure 2.2 completes the strategy that might be taken to reduce the stress from "too heavy a workload."

Productive professors learn to manage the causes of problems, not just mask their symptoms. While aspirin provides temporary relief, managing stressors produces permanent results. Before you take the quickest and easiest path to reduce your tension, try the Action Plan. It will help you successfully reduce your stress by controlling your problems rather than having them control you.

I. Most Bothersome Stress Event: Too heavy a workload, one that cannot be finished in a day.

II. CAUSES	II. SOLUTIONS	IV. SPECIFIC ACTION PLAN
1. Unrealistic appraisal of time	1. Conduct time schedules	a) The plan is to: Concentrate on high payoff tasks
2. Inability to say "no"	2. Gain assertive skills	b) Type of action
3. Overcommitted to work more than family	3. Set your family/job goals	☒ corrective ☐ preventive
4. Unclear delineation of responsibilities	4. Request specific Faculty Planning Guide	☐ interim ☐ contingent
5. Cannot distinguish between high and low priorities	5. Concentrate on high payoff tasks	☐ adaptive ☐ other

V. STEPS FOR IMPLEMENTATION

1. Activity: Develop high payoff and low payoff lists 3. How often: Daily for two weeks
2. Where: In the office at my desk with no interruptions 4. When: Every morning at 8:30 a.m.

VI. FOLLOW-UP EVALUATION

1. Did I write out my lists every morning? 3. Did I actually delegate or eliminate any low payoff tasks?
2. Were the high payoff tasks completed first? 4.

VII. NEGATIVE UNINTENDED CONSEQUENCES

1. My chair became upset with incomplete tasks important to him/her 3. I created an overload for my staff by delegating too many tasks to them
2. Work became too regimented and not as carefree 4.

MODIFICATIONS FOR PLAN NEEDED? Because my chair needs to know what I am concentrating on (high payoffs), I should communicate with him/her periodically to seek concurrence with my plan.

Figure 2.2. Faculty Action Plan

Institutional Strategies: Ideas for Intervention

Stress intervention programs that work well in one occupation have been found to have relatively little success in others (Caplan et al., 1980). While disciplines within universities potentially represent different occupations, when it comes to stress, faculty have more similarities than differences. Therefore, institutional strategies for stress management may be applicable across campus.

A caution, however, is noted: A doctor who knows the cure for many illnesses still cannot precisely prescribe the cure for a particular patient until careful diagnosis is completed. Examination must also be made within specific college and university settings before accurate prescriptions can be issued. Given this limitation, some general strategies for coping with the factors of faculty stress are proposed below (Gmelch, 1987) and summarized in Table 2.2.

Stress Factor 1: Reward and Recognition. With respect to insufficient and unclear *rewards*, goal-setting sessions should be undertaken to focus on your most productive activities. At a minimum, an annual meeting should be established with your department chair to address rewarded activities for the next year in teaching, research, and service. This meeting would assist you in defining a work plan for the area and activities on which you should concentrate for the next year. A sample of a Faculty Planning Guide can be found in Exercise 2.4.

Every faculty member should not be expected to produce excellence in teaching, research, and service every year, but possibly excellence in one and competence in the others. In this way, the established goals can also be discussed in relation to their congruence with departmental and university missions such that each faculty member, when combined with the faculty as a whole, represents a faculty productivity portfolio of excellence. Each is then rewarded for his or her contribution to the portfolio.

Table 2.2 Faculty Coping Techniques

Institutional Strategy	
1. Reward and Recognition	Reward
	a. goal identification and congruence
	b. faculty productivity portfolio
	Recognition
	c. news release
	d. departmental displays
	e. excellence awards
2. Time Constraints	Time management inservice
	a. identify HIPOS
	b. reduce LOPOS
	Efficient working environment
	c. central dictation and word processing
	d. screen telephone calls
	e. HIPO hideout
	f. effective planning and organization
3. Departmental Influences	Faculty participation based on following criteria:
	a. does it make a difference?
	b. adequate information?
	c. goal congruence?
4. Professional Identity	Recognize success is:
	a. independent of achievement
	b. aspiration-achievement gap
	Set annual goals with chair/dean
	Develop support networks
	Sponsor senior mentoring
5. Student Interaction	Faculty training in:
	a. counseling skills
	b. negotiation skills
	c. principled negotiation

Recognition has traditionally been viewed as monetary reward for excellence. However, numerous other mechanisms present powerful alternatives to financial benefit. The use of news releases on faculty activities; departmental bulletin boards displaying recent publications; and yearly faculty excellence awards in teaching, service, and research could be bestowed at the departmental level to ensure a more realistic recognition of many deserving faculty members rather than one member of the university singled out for excellence.

Stress Factor 2: Time Constraints. Paperwork, meetings, and interruptions represent not "ends" of academic productivity but the "means" to goal accomplishment. You should spring these stress traps so that you can effectively use your time to achieve your goals. In-service training in time management techniques may provide the logical remedy, not necessarily to provide you with training in new ideas, but to remind you of techniques already known and in need of more consistent practice. A few of the basic time management principles you should consider are:

1. Identify high payoff (HIPOS) activities which will help you attain excellence in teaching, research, and service.
2. Reduce your involvement in less meaningful, low payoff (LOPOS) activities by cutting back excessive meetings, committee work, and general administrivia.
3. Arrange your working environment so that telephone calls can be screened, recorded, or forwarded so your hours can be blocked into uninterruptible time.
4. Find a retreat or HIPO hideout (workroom or home office) where you can have uninterruptible time for class preparation, manuscript preparation, and other activities that require blocks of quiet time.
5. Develop effective self-management techniques and attitudes, particularly in planning and organizing, so that you can get the important things done, rather than just getting things done.

It is particularly ironic that institutions of higher education often ignore their most important resource by treating faculty as self-sufficient and not trainable once the terminal degree (Ph.D.) is achieved. Faculty development programs addressing such needs as time management can provide a great boost to both faculty morale and productivity.

Exercise 2.4
Faculty Planning Guide

Name: _____

Definition of Assignment

A. TEACHING

1. Formal Instruction

Fall		Spring	
Course Number & Title	Number of Students	Course Number & Title	Number of Students

2. Informal Instruction (e.g., TAs supervised, advising)
   Undergraduate Advising (Number)

Graduate Student Advising:
   Number of Master's Students
   Number of Doctoral Students
   Number of Master's Students at Project/Thesis Stage:
   Number of Doctoral Students at Dissertation Stage:
       (post prelims, May graduation):
   Number of CAP Students Advising:
   Other:

B. SCHOLARLY ACTIVITY

Focus of Scholarship: _____

_____

_____

1. Manuscripts (planned for, or in preparation—books, monographs, articles, papers)

   Title   Intended Audience/Journal

2. Research and Development Projects

   Title   Source of Support

3. Presentations

     Title   Audience

A. Original Presentations/
   Keynote Speeches

B. Secondary Presentations

4. Other Scholarly Activities

C. SERVICE
    1. National/International

    2. State/Regional

    3. Institutional/WSU

D. ADMINISTRATION (Projects, Grants, Programs)

E. PROFESSIONAL/PERSONAL DEVELOPMENT

Faculty Member	Date	Chair	Date

Exercise 2.4 Continued

Stress Factor 3: Departmental Influence. Faculty members blame much of their dissatisfactions on the institution's internal structure and their own limited involvement in planning and governance. Although departmental influences are among the most important features of faculty life, you should not lose sight of the fact that you probably want to influence decisions that affect you but do not desire a total participatory structure riddled with more committees and meetings. To assist you in determining your level of desired involvement, consider the range of approaches to decision making from "raise the issue and let faculty decide" to "let the department chair make the decision independently and then announce it to the faculty." Your participation should be decided using the following minimum criteria:

1. Does the issue under consideration make a difference to you?
2. Does the chair have adequate information to make a decision without your input?
3. Is there goal congruence between department and faculty desires?

If the answer to all the questions is "yes," then save yourself some time and energy and let the department chair make the decision. However, if your answer to question 1 is "yes" but "no" to questions 2 and 3, get involved in creating your own destiny. Remind your department chair that to share governance and responsibility by involving faculty in decision making can also reduce his or her stress and workload.

Stress Factor 4: Professional Identity. Many have postulated that the feeling of being productive is dependent on the relationship between one's achievement and one's level of aspiration, not on absolute productivity. It is crucial, therefore, that you have an opportunity to set your goals realistically. The primary cause of faculty stress is "excessively high self-expectations." If you can set a realistic agenda, not only will productivity be focused, but you will also be more satisfied with your accomplishments. Use the Faculty Planning Guide to articulate a realistic plan for yourself and communicate it to your chair for his or her assistance and appraisal.

Because younger faculty members, especially women and minorities, represent groups suffering most from professional identity stress, support networks, coaching, and mentoring systems should be provided to give the guidance and collegial support needed to gain understanding and acceptance of one's contribution to his or her profession.

Stress Factor 5: Student Interaction. Much of the stress involved in student interaction stems from its confrontation and conflict orientation. Training in counseling and negotiation skills is most important in this area. This training should not necessarily focus on soft negotiation skills, such as "how to become friends," or on hard techniques, such as "how to live with adversaries," but on the practices of principled negotiations in which faculty members, students, and chairs become problem solvers seeking wise outcomes efficiently and amicably (Fisher & Ury, 1990).

In summary, the majority of top faculty stressors relate directly to time pressures, resource constraints, reward structure, personal identity, and interaction with students, colleagues, and administrators. The previous tips for faculty stress traps are outlined in Table 2.2. Many of these techniques will receive greater attention and elaboration in the final chapter of this book on how to maintain your balance. Some stressors are clearly more controllable than others. Look to your chair for assistance with your stresses stemming from lack of resources and inadequate reward structures. Even in these more difficult areas, any effort you can make toward expanding your resources and reappraising your capabilities and limitations is worthwhile.

3 | Use the Power of Perception

When we are nervous, tense, or uptight, we normally attribute these conditions to outside forces rather than looking within ourselves. We have blamed academia for placing excessive demands beyond our capabilities when in actuality we self-impose probably 80% to 90% of our stress through our behavior, beliefs, and unrealistic goals.

Stress traps, as noted in Chapter 2, come from a myriad of sources. They represent a set of objective demands which can only become subjectively stressful in the way we perceive them. Perceptions, then, become the key to whether stress is received or denied at Stage 2 of your stress cycle. To understand this process, consider the following definition of stress:

> The anticipation of our inability to respond adequately to a perceived demand, accompanied by our anticipation of negative consequences for an inadequate response.

Let us analyze this definition word by word to provide greater insight into the role that perception plays in the stress cycle. *The anticipation* (which could be real or imaginary) *of our inability* (inability assumes we feel we do not have the skills) *to respond adequately* (response is Stage 3 of the stress cycle—the repertoire of coping responses we have available to meet the stressor) *to a perceived* (Stage 2 of the cycle and the

40

critical element in whether stress exists or not) *demand* (Stage 1 of the cycle, representing the list of potential stressors from Chapter 2), *accompanied by our anticipation* (again, anticipation could be real or imaginary) *of negative consequences* (Stage 4 and the result of an unhealthy stress cycle) *for an inadequate response* (inability to meet the challenges of stress).

This definition is based on our perceptions of our inability to meet the challenges of our job. However, this same perception that creates a negative stress response when we imagine we do not have the skills can easily be turned around into a positive one by merely looking at the potential stressor as a challenge we can meet. Stress then becomes defined as:

> Our anticipation of our ability to respond adequately to a perceived demand, accompanied by our anticipation of positive consequences for our adequate response.

Thus, it is how we approach faculty life that causes most of our stress. Our perceptions (Stage 2) play the major role in our resilience to, or acceptance of, stress in the academy. If we do not approach stress positively (as defined immediately above) the result in Stage 4 may be the negative consequences of mental and physical illness.

In this chapter you will consider the personalities, beliefs, and behaviors that affect your perception of and responses to stressors. You will (a) look at how some stress can be filtered out before it penetrates; (b) investigate who are the typical stressful professors; (c) look at your own personality to see if you are your own worst enemy; and (d) find ways to change your behaviors to become more effective. These inquiries are meant to pinpoint obstacles within, which can hold you back from success.

Faculty Stress Filters

What makes one day mild to one faculty member and traumatic to another? It depends essentially upon how we perceive

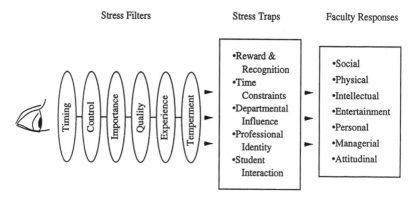

Figure 3.1. Faculty Stress Filters

each situation. Figure 3.1 outlines a stress filter model. The impact of a stressor trying to penetrate the professor in Stage 2 depends on how the professor views it through his or her own personalized filters. Much like looking at the world through special glasses, faculty use a polarizing filter to cut back bothersome glare, cool-green to temper the heat, red-hot to accentuate the important, and so on. Six filters are crucial in either enhancing or hampering your ability to handle stress: *timing, control, importance, quality, experience,* and *temperament.*

Coping is a process that requires *time.* A driver speeding through life seldom has time to effectively negotiate sudden turns, detours, or bumps along the road. The dawdler at the wheel has better use of peripheral vision and good judgment to evaluate alternative courses of action and to plan ahead.

Control serves as another filtering device. The more control over the duration and intensity of the stressor, the less stress created. Studies of commuters in the San Francisco Bay Area accentuate the relationship between stress and control. The most stressful event for one executive (measured by pulse rate) was not coping with the trials of business but driving to and from work—dodging cars, competing for position, getting caught in traffic—situations over which she had no control.

Therefore, it is not the magnitude of the stressor itself which seems to count but the amount of control one has over the stressor. How much control do you have over your faculty activities?

Another filter is the perceived *importance* of the event. For instance, if the potential stressor is irrelevant to your values or goals, its presence may not lead to feelings of frustration. However, if the stressor blocks satisfaction of an important goal, such as publishing a manuscript or securing a grant, stress will most probably ensue.

The *quality* of information you use to filter out stress acts as a stress diffuser. Researchers have found that increasing knowledge and information allows you to see a variety of ways to deal with difficulties. If your filter helps you focus on such information you see more alternatives from which to choose.

Many new, young, and underrepresented faculty may not have an important filter available to them: the *experience* senior professors have from which to view potentially troublesome situations. The newer the situation, the greater the reaction. If you have already encountered the problem of developing a course syllabus and publishing an article it may not be as stressful the second time around.

The final, and probably most important filter, is *temperament*, or our basic disposition. Martha Washington once remarked: "I am still determined to be cheerful and happy whatever the situation...for I have also learned from experience [the previous filter] that the greater part of our happiness or misery depends on our dispositions and not upon our circumstances." To a great extent, our stress reaction depends on our temperament or disposition for handling tension and anxiety. A great deal of research has been conducted to determine the relationship between different people's dispositions and consequent vulnerability to stress-related diseases. This will be the topic of discussion in the next section of this chapter.

In sum, there is more to the management of stress than meets the eye. You can place a set of filters before you to help polarize, refract, and diffuse attacking stressors. Your filters must be sound, continually maintained, and properly used so they remain cool to filter unnecessary stress from your life and job. Now let us look beyond the filters and find out who are the most likely victims of stress.

Who Is the Stressed Professor?

We will begin our exploration by examining the most likely faculty to experience stress. Are you stressed? If so, is it due to your current rank, tenure, gender, ethnicity, stage of life, or the behavior and personality you exhibit? Through self-examination, many myths we hold about "who is most stressed" will be exposed and either confirmed, dispelled, or left open to question.

Is It the Nature of Faculty Work?

The most popularized research on this question can be found in Table 3.1. The National Institute for Occupational Safety and Health published this list of the most and least stressful occupations. Since then the data have appeared in popular magazines and newspapers across the country with everyone searching to see if their occupation is among the most stressful. Review the list and you will discover the classic stress occupations such as doctors, dentists, police officers, executives, air traffic controllers, and other professionals are missing. These are curious omissions until you discover that the ranking of stressful occupations comes from a study only in the state of Tennessee, and is based upon death rates and admission records to hospitals and mental health facilities. Is Tennessee typical of the United States? Because more laborers than college professors die or have higher admissions rate to health facilities, are laborers more stressed?

Researchers are not always sure what makes certain occupations, such as laborer, secretary, or professor, stressful. University of Michigan researchers have generally concluded

Table 3.1 Occupational Stress

Professions With Most Stress (From most to least stress)
1. Laborer
2. Secretary
3. Inspector
4. Clinical Lab Technician
5. Office Manager
6. Foreman
7. Manager/Administrator
8. Waitress/Waiter
9. Machine Operator
10. Farm Owner
11. Miner
12. Painter

Professions With Least Stress (In order of increasing stress)
1. Clothing Sewer
2. Checker, Examiner
3. Stock Handler
4. Craft Worker
5. Maid
6. Farm Laborer
7. Heavy Equipment Operator
8. Freight Handler
9. Child-Care Worker
10. Package Wrapper
11. College Professor
12. Personnel Worker

SOURCE: From ranking of 130 occupations by the National Institute for Occupational Safety and Health

that jobs are particularly tense when employees do not have clear objectives, are torn between conflicting demands, have little control over decisions affecting them, have too much or too little to do, or are responsible for other people's professional development and careers. Sound like your job?

Several of these conditions accurately characterize how faculty often view themselves. In Chapter 2 you learned that faculty suffered from the stresses of having unclear rewards and recognition, feeling constrained by time, trying to influence decisions affecting them, dealing with their own professional identity, and working with students.

Another conclusion about occupational stress comes from a NASA study revealing that people responsible for managing others have higher stress (measured by higher blood pressure and nervous habits like smoking) than those responsible for things. Keep this broad generalization in mind as we look at what research has identified as stressful dispositions. The answer lies in the interaction between the individual and the occupation.

Does Stress Have a Gender? A Color?

It is a well-known fact that men suffer higher rates of alcoholism, ulcers, lung cancer, suicide, and heart disease than women. White women live nearly 8 years longer than white men, 14 years longer than black men; and black women live longer than black men. As the number of women in professional positions increases, so do the incidences of stress and stress-related diseases.

Many women have the double burden of returning home to a full workload. Remember from Chapter 2 that our stress studies found married women professors have more stress than men and single women both, from the stress factors of professional identity and time constraints (Gmelch, Wilke, & Lovrich, 1986). Several factors may account for these differences. First, women bear a greater responsibility than men for family tasks, a fact that serves to restrict the time that they have available to devote to professional activities. Also, male professions can usually call on their female companions to assist with clerical and routine tasks required in professional responsibilities; the same is seldom true for female professionals (Freeman, 1977). Similarly, there is evidence to suggest that female faculty generally serve on more committees and are more often assigned heavier teaching loads than their male counterparts (Koester & Clark, 1980). Finally, social mores in many settings still restrict female faculty from interaction with male colleagues, interactions that typically provide professional support, intellectual stimulation, and collaboration for research projects and professional activities (Kanter, 1977; Koontz, 1979). Tack and Patitu (1992) contend that

> women faculty members are less satisfied with their positions than their male counterparts. Today, women represent a small percentage of the faculty cohort, make lower salaries than their male colleagues, are found in lower professoral ranks, are often employed in part-time rather than full-time positions, represent disciplines typically reserved for females, work in less prestigious institutions, feel that their supervisors do not value their input, and are not tenured. (p. iv)

Similar conditions are found in higher education for minority faculty members; when compared with their white counterparts, they are less likely to be tenured, they receive lower salaries, have lower academic rank, and feel isolated and unsupported in the academy. Clearly, these problems must be addressed to recruit and retain minority facutly and to reduce the stress they experience in the academy.

Similarly, in a paired comparison study of black and white professors, black faculty perceived more stress in the area of rewards and recognition and showed significantly more stress from high self-expectations and more demand being placed on their time (Smith & Jordan, 1993).

Understanding the relationship between gender and ethnicity and stress in higher education is of growing importance. Twenty years ago only 13% of doctorates were being granted to women. Today, approximately 37% of doctorates are earned by women (Bowen & Schuster, 1986). Rosabeth Moss Kanter, in *Men and Women of the Corporation* (1977), sheds light on the significance numbers play in social support in organizations. As it applies to institutions of higher education, group support is impacted by the proportional representation of different kinds of faculty in a meeting, whether it be by race, gender, ethnicity, or any other significant influence. For example, "uniform" departments have only one kind of person and are considered homogeneous with respect to salient status. One might conjecture that most uniform departments are composed of white male faculty members. This numerically significant type, called "dominants," controls the department and its culture. At the other extreme, "skewed" departments are composed of a preponderance of one type over another, up to a ratio of perhaps 85 to 15. The few in a skewed department are called "tokens," are often treated as representatives of their category, as symbols rather than individuals. Even if a department has two tokens in a skewed group of faculty members, it is difficult for them to generate an alliance or significant support group to help with unique stresses.

The importance of having diverse participation in departments is not so much in the numbers or proportions they represent, but the perspective they bring to problems (Dillard, 1992). Minority faculty not only bring important role models for other minorities but also offer other models for handling stress. A stress-resistant department climate must have multiple perspectives.

Is Your Personality Causing You Stress?

Although it is difficult to establish clear causal links between personality factors and disease, sufficient research evidence exists to document the link between certain types of behaviors and heart disease, cancer, arthritis, asthma, migraine headaches, and other ailments. This evidence is too strong to dismiss and too critical to overlook.

Of particular importance and deserving immediate attention is the coronary heart disease personality, Type A, developed and documented by Drs. Friedman and Rosenman (1974) at Mt. Zion Hospital in San Francisco. Because heart disease remains the number-one killer in America, your attention to the information in Friedman and Rosenman's book, *Type A Behavior and Your Heart,* may save a life, perhaps your own.

Type As approach their jobs with intensity and impatience. For this reason, among others, they are attacked by heart disease at triple the rate of more relaxed and easygoing professors. But what exactly is Type A behavior? You may have heard about it before but how can you recognize it? Read the brief explanations to get a feel for the Type A professor. You may see a little of yourself, a colleague, or best friend in these descriptions.

Types of Behavior

The Raging Bull

The Raging Bull suffers inner turmoil. This pent-up aggression manifests itself in nervous tics, clenched fists, pounding tables, grinding teeth, and other outward clues of the inner struggles they endure. In faculty meetings they speak first, accentuate words in an explosive manner (at inappropriate times), and rush their thoughts, jumping from one (hidden) agenda to another.

In conversation with other faculty members, especially slow speaking, methodical Type Bs, Type As rush others and finish their sentences. They incessantly interrupt others. In fact, nothing is quite so annoying to Type A professors as to have someone go right on talking when they are interrupting.

The Harried Hurrier

Type A faculty feel impatient with the rate at which most things take place in colleges and universities. Repetitious reports and duties drive them crazy, as they only go around once in this world and don't have time for a second glance. They anguish over waiting for anything from the secretarial pool or department chair. Typical Type A professors at the supermarket buy 8 items or less so they can go through the "Type A line" (flashing lights, no checks), or if they have to buy 9 they will buy 29 and stock up for the month. Of course, that is still not good enough. When finished filling their baskets they rush to the checkout stands, count the number of people in each line, and before selecting the shortest line, glance at the cashier to see how efficient he or she looks (and, of course, to see if there is a bagger)—only to find everyone in line is writing checks.

This harried behavior contrasts the easygoing Type B shopper who carefully selects the items, finds one of many short lines, and while waiting, either turns to exchange greetings with a fellow shopper or takes a magazine from the rack to peruse. Once at the checkstand, the Type B puts the magazine back, saves a couple bucks, as well as his or her sanity, and strolls home.

The Indispensable Professor

Indispensability is a common trait of Type As. They believe success comes from getting things done faster than others. Therefore, they are afraid to slow down because others may get ahead. They end up scheduling more and more into their days in less and less time, and with fewer allowances for the unforeseen. Therefore any deviation or interruption becomes a major crisis because there is no time for it. Friedman suggests they usually engage in polyphasic behavior. That is, they do two or more things simultaneously: going over class lecture notes, talking on the phone, acknowledging a student's question, and eating lunch in the office, all at the same time. It used to be called efficiency, but now seems like lunacy. No one can do two or more mental things simultaneously and do them well. As a wise hunter once said: "Never chase two rabbits at once."

The Incessant Time Racer

A classic trait of Type As is time urgency. They try to do too much in too short a time. Even though all professors have 24 hours in a day, it is never enough for the Type A. There is no time to become the things worth *being* because they are preoccupied with getting the things worth *having*. They play the numbers game—the number of articles published, students advised, acquaintances accumulated, and so on. It is not the quality of their academic productivity, but the quantity.

Time is of the essence so they feel guilty when they relax, even for a few minutes. They eventually die from what Friedman calls "hurry sickness": lack of boredom. Everyone needs a little boredom and Type As never give themselves the chance. They are no longer able to observe the lovely things in life: the seasons passing, the trees blooming, the leaves turning colors. Instead, the Type A notices that it is time to place raking leaves on the "to do" list again.

Type As eat, walk, and talk at a fast pace. Getting more words in per minute may be efficient, but the trouble with people who talk too fast is that they often say something they haven't thought of yet.

The Aggressive Competitor

The final portrayal of a Type A professor is the aggressive competitor. This is not to say competition is unhealthy. We all know competing goads us on to success and peaks our performance. However, the Type A engages in relationships not with good, clean, competition in mind, but with winning—that's what counts. They say that if games are not for winning, why do we keep score? In fact, if one Type A meets another in the faculty room, it is not with a sense of compassion, but competition.

In faculty social settings, Type As play the power corners of the room, trying to get people talking about subjects within their expertise. If they lose the interest of one group they move to the next power corner and espouse another topic of personal wisdom. In fact, some Type As become so extreme in their competition they cannot even allow their children to beat them in a game of checkers.

In sum, Type A professors can be characterized as overly competitive achievers, aggressive, fast working, impatient, restless, hyperalert, explosive in speech, tense, always feeling under pressure, and, according to Friedman's recent studies, insecure and aware of their own limitations. In contrast, Type B behavior is the mirror opposite: relaxed, easygoing, seldom impatient, taking more time to enjoy things in life besides work, not easily irritated, working steadily, seldom lacking time, not preoccupied with social achievement, and moving and speaking more slowly.

Who Are the Type A Professors?

Many of our preconceived notions suggest that Type A is the American way of life, from the legacy of the Puritan work ethic to the successes of our economic existence. After all, don't higher educational institutions encourage ambition, drive, indispensability, competitiveness, and immediacy—all of which reinforce the workaholic and Type A traits? However, Type A behavior poses a major threat to the university's well-being.

Let us explore who the Type A professors are. Are they more successful than Type Bs? Although most research links Type A behavior and coronary heart disease, we are beginning to also understand who, demographically, are the Type As. Typically, they are male, middle class, middle-aged, and offsprings of Type A parents. They work longer work weeks, travel more days per year, work in high growth or rapid decline organizations, have supervisory responsibility for people, have heavy workloads, work in a competitive environment, and have conflicting demands on their job.

The propensity for professors to be Type A is too real to ignore. As you can see from Table 3.2, of the 23 occupations studied by the University of Michigan, professors rank sixth in exhibiting Type A behavior and third in overtime worked, right behind physicians and administrative professors (deans, chairs, etc.). On a positive note, only 4% of the professors reported coronary heart disease (Column 2), almost one third

Table 3.2 Influences on Occupational Stress

Occupation	(1) Type A	(2) Cardiovascular Disease	(3) Hours Work/Week
Administrative Professor	155	12.0%	56.4
Physician	149	12.5%	58.4
Tool & Die	123	14.3%	46.9
Administrator	111	8.3%	48.7
Blue Collar Supervisor	108	4.8%	47.6
Scientist	106	5.1%	46.6
Professor	106	4.1%	51.6
Air Traffic Controller	102	3.7%	38.1
Train Dispatcher	98	9.3%	41.7
White Collar Supervisor	95	4.8%	43.7
Air Traffic Controller (Sm)	94	0.0%	38.7
Electronic Technician	93	9.7%	40.2
Policeman	89	2.7%	46.1
Forklift Driver	87	10.9%	40.4
Courier	85	5.0%	39.1
Assembler (nonpaced)	84	5.8%	41.9
Engineer	82	5.5%	43.3
Machine Tender	81	5.9%	42.9
Accountant	74	12.0%	40.6
Assembler, Relief	74	3.7%	40.5
Programmer	69	4.4%	42.2
Cont In Flow	67	11.9%	40.8
Assembler (machine paced)	63	1.3%	41.1

less than administrative professors (Caplan, et al., 1980). Who said life in the academy was easy?

Who Are Most Productive?

You still probably want to know the bottom line: Are Type As more productive than Type Bs? The Type B professor has just as much ambition and drive as the Type A, but the Type B drive employs a steady, confident, and secure approach toward academics rather than a goading, irritating, and infuriating one. Type B considers alternatives and takes time to think the issues through before reacting. The Type A's restless, hostile, hyperalert, and hasty work pattern may not win them promotion or tenure. Together they both represent ambition, drive, and self-assurance; only the path and method differ. On their path, the Type As get caught in a double bind. Their restless behavior increases the likelihood of exposure to certain stresses like overload, while at the same time their refusal to relax and slow down decreases their resistance to stress. The low stress mode of Type B is more conducive to health maintenance through a more contemplative, tempered life-style based on an inner sense of calmness. Thus, Type As create excessive stress for themselves while their equally ambitious Type Bs approach their job in a more relaxed fashion.

What Is the Winning Combination?

What about a Type A working in a Type B college, or a Type B working in a Type A college? Just as individuals may exhibit Type A or Type B behaviors, universities and colleges can be A or B with respect to their environment, climate, and culture.

If we try to find the best fit between the disposition of the faculty member and the institution what would it be? Are Type As better off in a Type A or a Type B institution? Where are they most productive? Where are they least productive? Where would you like to work? Where would you perform best? Least?

One might conjecture that the highest levels of stress exist where an improper fit exists between the individual and organization: Type As working in a Type B department and Type Bs working in a Type A department. Or might it be that Type As, no matter where they work, will create the greatest stress, for themselves and their departments.

Can You Type Your Behavior?

Are you Type A? Do you characteristically exhibit Type A traits? Answer the questions in Exercise 3.1 to find out. Better yet, ask your spouse or colleague to answer the questions for you. Assessing your own personality is seldom accurate. Friedman believes that because so many Type A individuals rationalize their own behaviors seldom can they type themselves honestly. They deny their Type A traits because they see them as signs of normal, healthy, vibrant living.

The best method for deciphering behavior types is the structured interview in which individuals are asked questions similar to those in Exercise 3.1. Their answers would only provide the first clue since a trained interviewer observes the behaviors exhibited as the questions are asked. The interviewer would state: "When you go on a vacation do you always . . . ," then pause to see if the interviewee would jump in with impatient expressions like "uh-huh, uh-huh, you mean . . . ," or even finish the question for the interviewer. Other clues would be rapid eye movements, odd posture, knee jiggling, facial tautness, and explosive speech patterns. Without the clinical assistance of a trained interviewer, take the second best method for determining behavior type and ask a close friend his or her honest impressions.

Type A and Type B faculty are dichotomized characteristically as polar opposites; one is hurried, get-ahead, and competitive while the other is relaxed, easygoing, and secure. While they appear to be polar opposites, for a more practical interpretation the types should be considered on a continuum from A to B. On the continuum below, place an X that corresponds with your score in Exercise 3.1.

A-1			A-2		B-3				B-4
20	18	16	14	12	10	8	6	4	2	1

(Number of "Yes" answers)

Exercise 3.1
Type A Faculty Behavior
Answer the following questions indicating what *most often* applies to you:

Yes	No		
___	___	1.	Do you hate to wait in line at the bookstore or bank?
___	___	2.	Do you frequently try to do several things at the same time?
___	___	3.	Are you generally dissatisfied with what you have accomplished as a professor?
___	___	4.	Do you enjoy competition and feel you always have to be the best in your field?
___	___	5.	When your colleagues speak slowly do you find yourself trying to rush them along by finishing the sentence for them?
___	___	6.	Do you become impatient when someone does their work slowly?
___	___	7.	When engaged in conversation do you usually feel compelled to tell others about your own interests or areas of expertise?
___	___	8.	Do you become irritated when something is not done exactly right?
___	___	9.	Do you rush through your tasks to get them done as quickly as possible?
___	___	10.	Do you feel you are constantly under pressure to get more done?
___	___	11.	In the past few years, have you taken less time for your vacations?
___	___	12.	While listening to other people, do you ususally find your mind wandering to other tasks and subjects?
___	___	13.	When you meet aggressive colleagues do you usually feel compelled to compete with them?
___	___	14.	Do you tend to talk fast in regular conversation and/or during your lectures?
___	___	15.	Are you too busy being a professor to have time for avocations and outside activities?
___	___	16.	Do you seek and need recognition from your chair and peers?
___	___	17.	Do you take pride in working best "under pressure"?
___	___	18.	Do you feel compelled to do most things in a hurry?
___	___	19.	Are you usually the first one done with a meal?
___	___	20.	Is it difficult for you to relax, even for a few hours?

Positions A-1 and B-4 represent the extreme Type A and Type B individuals. Few of us fall into either extreme position. Where did your score fall? Are you a strict Type A in the A-1 position? If so, Friedman has bad news. He has yet to change a Type A person to any shade of B unless he or she has first had a heart attack. In other words, the Type A pattern is so ingrained that it requires strong motivation to overcome.

If you have classified yourself as A-1 in Exercise 3.1, do not let this fact cause you heart failure. Remember, self-assessment is seldom totally accurate and should be followed up by a trained physician or clinician.

For all the rest of us who are A-ish, there are many techniques we can use to become shades of B if we choose. First, review the questions in Exercise 3.1 where you indicated "yes," a sign of a Type A trait. Ask yourself the simple question, "Do I want to change?" Is this trait detrimental to me, my colleagues, my relationship with my friends and family? If the answer is "yes" then write in the space next to the question a simple technique to begin changing that part of your behavior.

For example, if you tend to speak so rapidly that students have a hard time understanding your lectures, remind yourself 20 times a day to "speak slowly." Use any gimmick that works. For instance write "speak slowly" on a piece of paper and put it in your pocket or purse. Every time you put your hand in your pocket during your lecture or other times during the day (dozens of times for most of us) you feel that piece of paper and automatically remind yourself to speak slowly. Carry the paper with you for a few weeks and you will find a change in your speech pattern. Once you form habits, they will help form you. The final section provides techniques helpful in modifying Type A behaviors. You cannot change your personality overnight, but if you have the willpower, you can incrementally correct some unwanted Type A habits.

Race Horses

The previous section explored the negative, Type A behaviors that can cause you discomfort, disability, or even premature death. Type As are stressed professors. We also know a great number of colleagues who actually thrive on pressure and rarely fall ill. What distinguishes those who succumb to stress from those who survive, and even thrive on it?

Research in this area is in its infancy, however the attention given to the ills of stress has created an equal fervor to investigate the strength of stress. Dr. Hans Selye (1974), a prominent stress expert who introduced the word *stress* 40 years ago, believed there has been too much attention given to overwork, excessive striving, and even Type A behavior. Instead, he felt we should find the level of stress that suits us best. Some faculty are "race horses": Only happy with vigorous, fast-paced life-styles, they thrive on stress.

Others are "turtles" who need peace, quiet, and a restful environment. A self-pronounced race horse himself, Selye believed the real danger occurred when you push yourself beyond what you can normally endure. No self-assessment instrument can establish your endurance level. You have to develop an instinctive sensitivity that alerts you when you are running above or below your best stress intake.

The Hardy Professor

A few clues have recently emerged regarding psychological qualities that may account for resilience to stress. Dr. Suzanne Kobasa began by studying the health of 670 middle to upper managers (Kobasa & Maddi, 1980). She found managers with high stress but low illness were more actively involved in their work and social lives; they believed they were in more control of the events in their lives; and they viewed change as a challenge. Drs. Kobasa and Maddi followed up by studying 259 executives for two years and reconfirmed that those most resilient to stress used three protective factors: challenge, commitment, and control. Let's explore each of the three Cs for guarding against excessive faculty stress.

1. *Challenge.* Hardy professors see problems as an opportunity or a challenge. This challenge, however, is not met without restraint. Hardy professors are willing to take risks, though not excessive risks, and do not lack persistence in meeting challenge. They transform change to their advantage—thus reducing their own stress level.

2. *Commitment.* Hardy professors have the ability to commit to their discipline and to their personal life. They become active and interested in life's opportunities. They are more likely to identify the important aspects of life and commit themselves to these aspects to obtain goals.

3. *Control.* Hardy professors would like to believe they can affect their work environment. Rather than think stress will kill them, they take charge and choose among various courses of action to diffuse threatening stressful events.

In summary, hardy professors are those who are involved and committed, who believe they control their own lives, and who see change as an opportunity rather than a threat. Several national studies on college and university faculty find that despite the stress, faculty on the whole remain committed, dedicated, resourceful, and resilient (Bowen & Schuster, 1986).

The hardy professor and race horse typologies are probably embraced heartily by many. Some researchers take exception to tagging Type A as the real culprit and argue that hostility and cynicism are even more lethal. No matter what the argument, the evidence surrounding Type A behavior and heart disease, cancer personalities, and other connections between disposition and illness should not be rationalized and dismissed. Our enthusiastic acceptance of pressure, competition, and tension strikingly contrasts the alarm expressed by research scientists, organizational psychologists, cardiologists, and psychiatrists.

Coping With Your Personality

Now that we know that we endure stress, how do we get rid of it? We usually do one of two things when faced with such a problem: (a) develop the technology to control it, or (b) consult the experts in the field and model their behavior.

We can develop a technology by generating information about a phenomenon in order to make it a controlled, exact, and predictable hard science. Essentially, the Faculty Action Plan in Chapter 2 provides you with a mechanism for dealing with the stress traps you can control. However, there is not a tried and true technology for coping with all your stress; there are no blueprints that will serve all of us. Coping also should be viewed as an art: highly individualistic and personalized. Therefore, coping should not be reduced to a technology but seen as an opportunity. That is what makes coping exciting.

The experts can write with insight about these problems because many have already been there. A dozen ideas on healthful behaviors have been culled from the advice of Dr. Friedman and other experts. Because coping is an individual art, some techniques will work for you and others won't. They do not represent all-encompassing answers but incremental modifications to reduce stressful behaviors. Test them and test others until you develop you own repertoire of effective coping techniques.

1. *Plan a little idleness in each day.* The need for relaxation may not always coincide with a lunch break at the student union. Plan a little idleness in your day—morning, noon, and night. Rise 15 minutes earlier so you can read leisurely, exercise, or stroll, rather than gulp down a glass of juice and dash off to work. At noon take a midday walk to clear your mind, visit a museum, or exercise at the university gym to break the stress cycle. At night, stay in your office a half hour later to plan the next day and avoid rush hour traffic.

2. *Listen without interruption.* Be a good listener and a short answerer. We were given two ears and one mouth and ought to use them in that proportion. Hearing is not listening; hearing is a physical activity and listening is an intellectual one. In fact, if you are really listening to students or to your colleagues then you cannot be thinking about your own problems.

3. *Read a concentration book.* Although professors take home their journals, technical papers, and reports to read at night, you may be better off leaving your academic life behind you and getting involved in a "concentration" book to escape the academic-workaholic cycle. Read a book in which you can truly get lost. It could be a mystery or a historical novel. In fact, carry it around with you and when you find yourself becoming stressed by long lines or delays, lose your frustrations in your book.

4. *Compartmentalize work and nonwork activities.* One of the most difficult things for us to do is to leave our academic work at the end of the day. We need to compartmentalize or separate our work from our home life and make a distinction between the two. We realize that most professors work on the average of 52 hour weeks. However, attempt to compartmentalize your work both at home and in the academy so you can break out of the stress cycle.

5. *Have a retreat at home.* Everyone should have some place where he or she can be alone. You need to be able to get away, relax, and think without interruption—without anyone making demands on your time and attention. This is particularly important for professors who have a hard time leaving their professional work. Privacy is just as necessary as work, sleep, and food.

6. *Know your stress points.* Each of us is an individual. We are influenced by heredity, predisposition, past experience,

and the expectations placed on us by our colleges and departments. Our bodies are unique and react to stress in very personal ways. Everyone has some chronic tic that signals when she or he is under too much stress, whether it be a backache, headache, tight neck muscles, or a peptic ulcer. It is important for us to know what the early warning signals of stress are and use these bodily cues to signal time-out for stress breaks.

7. *Do not structure your leisure time.* If you presently structure your vacations by the hour so they resemble the movie *If It's Tuesday, This Must Be Belgium* (13 countries in 12 days), you may never return to work. Break down the structure and plan a little idleness into your leisure time. Ironically, the busiest time for marriage counselors and psychologists is in September, after the family's "restful" vacation. In fact, most families cannot spend more than 72 hours together without a major blowup due to structured vacations. While on vacation, live by your calendar, not your watch.

8. *Strive to enrich yourself.* A survey of 4,000 professionals found that less than 40% of them have any meaningful activity outside of work. Coping with stress is a multipronged attack. Therefore we need to take a holistic approach toward personal enrichment: physical, mental, spiritual, and emotional. Too often we treat the body without regard for the mind. Proper stress management means engaging in physical conditioning, mental stimulation, spiritual enlightenment, and emotional maturation.

9. *Seek the humor in life.* While tranquilizers represent the number-one prescription drug in our country, our built-in tranquilizer is humor. William Glasser (1976) comments that "fun frees the mind." Try to view your college from a new perspective. In a crisis situation, for instance, a little levity tends to calm the emotions and helps one find new and creative solutions for academic problems.

10. *Do one task at a time.* The Type A individual eats, walks, and talks at a very fast pace, engaging in what has been termed *polyphasic behavior*—that is, doing two or more things simultaneously. You can do effectively only one thing at a time, so select the most important task and do it first. Proceed step-by-step in descending order from the most important task to the least. If you worry about all the classes to prepare and manuscripts to publish, you will be preoccupied with stress.

11. *Manage your time before others do.* Of the stressors faced by professors, none is as pervasive as time. Setting time aside daily for the organization and planning of tasks helps substitute periods of contemplative thought and academic preparation in place of fragmented, unproductive time. Other techniques that control the open door paradox, the constant telephone interruptions, and the drop-in visitors can also be helpful.

A parody on Ecclesiastes, by Dr. Kenneth A. Erickson (and adapted to the academic setting), eloquently addresses this theme.

A Parody on Ecclesiastes
For every professor there is a season:
A time for students, and a time for the dean;
With time for some planning or the day's a scream;
A time to read mail, but more time to discard;
A time for "time-off" when the stress is too hard;
A time for crises, and a time for breaks;
A time to achieve, and a time for mistakes;
A time for committees (if agendas they'll hone);
A time to take calls and ignore the phone;
A time to decide, and a time for no decision;
A time for the open door, and a time for its opposition;
A time for your doing, and a time for delegation;
A time for dawdling, and a time for deep thinking;
A time to come to work, and a time to go;
A time to say yes, and times to say no;
A time to give praise for work that you see;
And time to be spent by yourself, stress-free.

12. *Be an androgynous professor.* Usual solutions to Type A behavior and stress include emphasis on proper nutrition, regular exercise, and changing life-styles. Another method suggested by A. G. Sargent (1980) is androgyny—a combination of Greek words *andro* for male and *gyn* for female. Masculinity and femininity are complementary, not opposite, domains of trait and behavior. Men and women should be both sensitive and tough, strong and gentle, emotional and rational and so on. Thus, androgyny means combining male and female behaviors approved by society that will allow us to act as individuals rather than stereotypes—to express and embrace all aspects of our personalities. We have become the slaves of male or female behaviors without the freedom to call upon the full repertoire of human behavior available to us.

Although the above 12 suggestions are varied, they all have something in common: *action.* Stress occurs when no action is taken. So take the time to act now and change your behavior. Stress is what you make of it. It can mean the difference between coping and collapsing. The secret of successful coping is not avoiding stress but challenging it. Whether you are exhausted or relaxed depends on how you perceive the stresses of the professoriate.

4 | Balance Your Personal and Professional Pressures

Alice: Will you tell me please, which way I ought to go from here?
Cheshire Cat: That depends a good deal on where you want to get to.
Alice: I don't care much.
Cheshire Cat: Then it doesn't matter which way you go!

Lewis Carroll

Work, for many academics, is their entire life. The role of professor gives you a title and self-concept that often dictate who you socialize with, where you live, how long you live there, and what life-style you have. Obviously, academia plays an important part in your life and provides you with pleasures as well as pressures. More than 60% of the stress faculty experience comes from their academic lives, not from their home and personal lives. As you may recall from Chapter 2, one of the top faculty stressors is participating in work related activities outside of regular working hours—and because faculty work on the average more than 55 hours per week, more than half of their waking hours are consumed by work. Ask yourself, "Who am I?" In answer to this question, most of you would describe yourself as a professor. But how many of you have other identities besides your professoriate? Do you have meaningful activities outside of the academy? Are you also an artist, author, sailor, gourmet cook, gardener, or sports enthusiast?

Personal and Professional Trade-offs

Your ability to develop a holistic life-style depends on how well you can make trade-offs between your professorial and personal time and interests. Consider the following properties and strategies for making trade-offs (Gmelch, 1991). A personal or professional trade-off is defined as *an exchange of one interest in return for another; especially, a giving up of something desirable.* In essence, life is a trade-off, yet success depends in large measure on making effective trade-offs. In your role as a faculty member, have you been able to keep a balance among your teaching, research, and service roles in addition to finding a balance between these professional roles and your personal goals?

Trade-offs: Balancing Time and Stress

One of the prices professors must pay for their autonomy is the open-ended nature of their time commitment. Because time is inelastic and irreplaceable, you must trade off some faculty time for personal time. Keep your personal goals in mind as you consider the professorial trade-offs elaborated below and in Exercise 4.1 (Gmelch & Miskin, 1993).

1. *Trade-offs act much like a ledger; a professor cannot debit one side without crediting the other.* As professors assume additional responsibilities and activities, the credits added to one side of the ledger must be debited against the other. In other words, if you decide to add another course to your teaching load, the time must come from one of your other faculty responsibilities and/or your personal time. Time resembles a "zero-sum" game—everyone has 24 hours in a day, no less and no more.

2. *Trade-offs between professional and personal interests vie for the same resources.* You experience excessive stress when the resources of time, energy, and commitment exist in limited supply. For example, this occurs when professionally related

travel to a national conference conflicts with spending the holidays with friends and family.

3. *Too many trade-offs in one direction create an imbalance and lead to negative stress.* Take a minute to indicate on the scale below the percent of the stress in your life that results from your position as a professor.

....
0   10   20   30   40   50   60   70   80   90   100%

When this question was asked of 1,200 faculty in all disciplines across America, they perceived that 60% of the stress in their lives came from their jobs. While Chapter 2 primarily focused on resolving the 60% stress from academic sources, you should not ignore the other 40% created by pressures away from the job for two important reasons. First, your effectiveness depends somewhat on your ability to handle pressures from your private life; second, professors need to approach their life-styles holistically, trading off effectively between their personal and profession goals. In other words, in order to be an effective academic you need to be an effective person—parent, spouse, public servant, and colleague. You cannot be unhealthy or ineffective in your private life and remain an effective professional. In order to succeed you must find the balance between your private and professional needs.

4. *Routine trade-off decisions usually favor the urgent over the important.* Daily pressures and stresses usually result in the tyranny of the urgent. Although urgent, these tasks may not represent the important points of your job. Due to their sense of urgency they receive immediate attention, leaving important responsibilities in imbalance. In the same spirit, many relatively unimportant tasks creep into your personal time as well unless you protect your calendar. Just as you take your professional calendar home and announce time commitments

to your family and friends, take your personal calendar to work and protect your personal commitments. For example, write your dates for season tickets to plays, performances, and sports events on your work calendar so you do not create a scheduling conflict.

5. *Trade-offs change with age, position, tenure, maturity, health, and time.* Think back to your first year as an assistant professor. The scales usually tip in favor of the professorial role until you become well rooted or established in your profession and discipline. Only after you begin to settle in and adapt to what you believe is most important in your role as faculty member do you become comfortable in your position. Of course, this will change over time with tenure, promotion, and experience.

6. *Professors cannot always control their trade-off decisions.* Deans, chairs, other faculty members, family, and friends dictate some rules that become immutable conditions in your life. It is not always possible to trade off a weekday morning of writing at home for late evenings in the office. Nor may noon racquetball games be willingly traded off for meetings. Unfortunately you do not always control the time and the agenda of meetings.

7. *Professors cannot always predict the consequences of trade-offs.* The need to teach evening classes for your students, to attend professional conferences to present papers, and to be available to your clientele represent professionally rewarding opportunities. However, they will also have consequences for your personal life that you should keep in mind and balance.

8. *The clearer the distinction and separation between personal and professional goals—and among teaching, research, and service goals—the fewer the potential conflicts between their trade-offs.* Establish goals in your personal and academic lives, and attempt to treat them as separate but equal entities. The next

section of this chapter will aid you in successfully accomplishing this goal.

9. *Trade-off decisions continue to favor one side or the other unless goals are established and updated periodically.* Without goals or objectives to guide professors in making trade-off decisions, the inertia of activities dominating one side of the scale can engulf all of your energy and time. Goals should be laid out for the semester or year rather than itemizing activities on a daily basis. Remember, without balance you may (a) find yourself sorely outdated in your discipline, or (b) reach the end of your professional career out of touch with important personal interests. Take a minute and jot down your personal and professional activities to see if they are in balance.

Just as the department requires strategic direction, periodically everyone needs to sit back and reflect on where they are going and how they plan to get there. Otherwise you will be caught up in the personal "activity trap," so enmeshed in activity that you forget what life is really all about. The activity becomes an end in itself. To break out of the trap, goals must be written and used to guide you like a map. As management expert George Odiorne (1974) cautions, "If you aim at nothing, you will hit it!"

Spend just one hour and complete the following set of exercises in this chapter. Your personal and career planning process consists of three parts: (a) lining up your professional career, (b) identifying your critical spheres of life, and (c) setting your professional aspirations and goals. Together they provide an integrated pattern for your professional and personal life.

Lining Up Your Professional Career

The past helps shape the future. You need to gain a perspective on the past in order to know what you may wish to follow in the future. Developing a professional career pattern in this

Exercise 4.1
Properties of Trade-offs

Review the properties of trade-offs, then list below the personal and professional activities you engage in and see if your personal and professional lives are in balance the way you desire.

(1) Trade-offs are like a ledger
(2) Trade-offs vie for the same resources
(3) Trade-offs create pressure - and relieve it
(4) Trade-off decisions favor the urgent
(5) Trade-offs change with age, tenure. . .
(6) Trade-offs cannot always be controlled
(7) Trade-off consequences cannot be predicted
(8) Trade-off distinction leads to less conflict
(9) Trade-offs favor one side or the other -
    unless goals are established

Balancing Your Trade-offs

Private   Professional

_____   _____
_____   _____
_____   _____
_____   _____
_____   _____
_____   _____
_____   _____

Exercise 4.2
Lining Up Your Professional Life

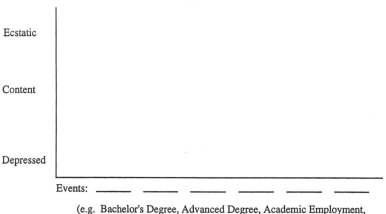

Ecstatic

Content

Depressed

Events: _____ _____ _____ _____ _____ _____

(e.g. Bachelor's Degree, Advanced Degree, Academic Employment,
Tenure, Promotion . . .)

section will provide you with this perspective. The left-hand corner of the baseline in Exercise 4.2 represents the beginning of your academic career, your entry into higher education. Begin with either the granting of your master's or doctoral degree or your first employment in higher education. The vertical line from that point expresses how you feel about your professional career on a continuum from satisfied to dissatisfied. Halfway up the vertical line is the neutral point; here you are neither ecstatic nor depressed, satisfied nor dissatisfied, just content. From this neutral point begin to draw your line.

Draw your line across the page from left to right (entry into academe to current position). Indicate by the configuration of your line how you feel about your life. Your line can be slanted, jagged, straight, curved, convoluted, or whatever shape expresses your feelings. It is a subjective analysis of how you feel about your career.

As an aid to lining up your professional career, Figure 4.1 portrays the typical career pattern of faculty, or what some may contend is a lack of career pattern. Some clues and consolations

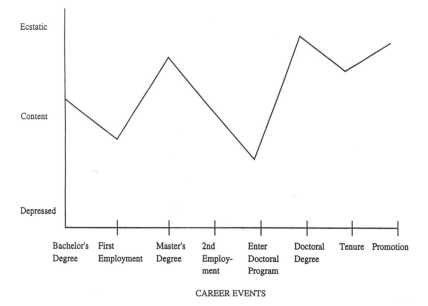

Figure 4.1. Faculty Career Pattern

might be helpful to explain the configuration of a faculty member's life, especially the peaks and valleys.

❶ *Valleys.* With most changes in life, whether good or bad, anticipated or unanticipated, there are usually corresponding dips and peaks in our excitement and energy. A productive professor forced to serve in an administrative capacity may even temporarily fall into a "valley of despair" until he or she is able to climb out.

❷ *Peaks.* The bestowing of a doctorate, passage from assistant to associate professor, granting of tenure, and gaining a full professorship all represent predictable peak periods for academics.

❸ *Patterns.* Besides predictable seven year transitions or rites of passage between professorial ranks, many professors experience cyclical patterns resembling three or five year itches, questioning whether there is life outside the academy.

❹ *Forces.* Some directions lifelines take cannot be controlled, but are left to external influences such as tenure review committees, extramural funding sources, and unfortunately, social, ethnic, and gender inequities.

❺ *Slope.* Finally, stand back and look at the general slope of your line. For a moment ignore the peaks and valleys and look at the direction your line is moving. Does your line keep climbing positively toward the upper right-hand corner of the graph, or drop down negatively toward the lower right-hand corner? In other words, is academics getting better with age or do you find yourself heading toward a less exciting and possibly dull existence?

The final section on career planning will either reinforce your positive direction or assist in turning your negatively sloped line toward the positive experiences in career advancement. But first, consider the spheres of your professional as well as your personal life. The question you must answer is: *In what spheres of my life should I set my goals?* In order to become a holistic professor you must balance the personal and professional parts of your career.

Balancing Spheres of Life

The second question you will need to answer is: *In what spheres of my professional and personal life should I set goals?* Remember, to become a holistic professor means balancing your personal life with your professional life. Figure 4.2 displays the areas of your personal life, segmented into your interests in physical health, mental health, family and friends, social needs, spiritual needs, and personal avocations. With respect to your professional sphere of life, it seems logical to segment your faculty responsibilities into three competing areas: teaching, scholarship, and service. Your ability to develop a holistic life-style depends on how well you can establish goals within each of these spheres as well as balance your energy and interests between the spheres.

Researchers discovered that those most fulfilled in their lives found their satisfaction in a combination of areas. However, if individuals were unrealistic in trying to attain too

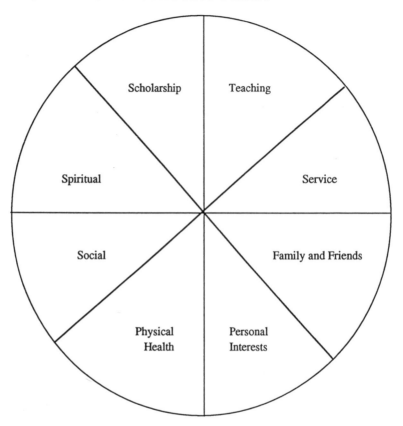

Figure 4.2. Your Professional and Personal Life

many conflicting goals and failed, they became dissatisfied, even in the areas where they had success. In other words, even if they missed the mark in just one sphere of their lives, this dissatisfaction would carry over into the other areas, causing an imbalance in their overall life fulfillment.

Therefore, the key to goal setting is to select areas needing attention. In many areas you probably have already taken corrective action and made progress. However, for now, reflect on each area: first, the importance each area plays in your personal life or professional progress; second, your current satisfaction with the progress in this area. If you are dissatisfied in some of the more important areas, be sure to address these first. For example, if you identified yourself more as a researcher than a teacher, but find you have less time to engage in scholarship activities, then write "scholarship interests" in the space marked *Professional Goal Area* in Exercise 4.3. In the same vein, if you find that the sedentary requirements of your scholarship have deprived you of time for physical activity then write "physical health" in the *Personal Goal Area.* Now you are ready to begin the third part of the career planning exercise.

Setting Professional/Personal Aspirations and Goals

Take one goal area at a time, such as physical health, and generate a number of goals that will help satisfy your need in each area. Do not limit your thinking at this point, but generate a number of possibilities. Then follow the steps below to focus your thinking in a few important areas.

❶ *Select goals.* You probably will have more goals than you could reasonably attain. To get started you will want to concentrate your energy on a few vital goals in each area. Select one or two goals in each area, but no more than seven to nine overall. Personal planning studies reinforce the notion that people cannot remember, process, and accomplish any more than seven to nine goals during one period of time.

Review your list of goals in Exercise 4.3 and place an asterisk next to one or two goals in each area that you wish to accomplish within your planning time frame—next term or semester, next academic year, or whatever time frame you have chosen.

❷ *Generate goal activities.* Write these seven to nine goals at the top of Exercise 4.4. Since goals cannot be "done," your next task is to break each of your goals into specific activities you can do to accomplish them. For example, if you have been away from the research side of the enterprise while serving in administrative capacities, one of your goals might be to return to your scholarship. Some of the

Exercise 4.3
Goal Identification*

Period beginning _____, ending _____	
(1) Professional Goal Area:	(2) Personal Goal Area:
Goals:	Goals:
a. _____	a. _____
b. _____	b. _____
c. _____	c. _____
d. _____	d. _____
e. _____	e. _____
f. _____	f. _____
g. _____	g. _____
h. _____	h. _____
i. _____	i. _____
j. _____	j. _____

SOURCE: Adapted for Walter H. Gmelch, Beyond Stress to Effective Management, John Wiley & Sons, New York, pg. 190.

activities you might identify are: focusing on writing themes, working with your colleagues on a new course, beginning a manageable research project, or simply finding time to write and read. In contrast, one of your personal management goals might be to become a better manager of your time. You may feel this is important because time pressure creates most of your stress; plus the more time you save on the teaching side of the job the less trading off you will have to do with your personal, or academic, interests. The activities you identify for better time management might include attending time management seminars, reading a book on time effectiveness, starting the day by prioritizing, boycotting needless meetings, saying no,

Exercise 4.4
Goal Activities

GOAL STATEMENTS

1._____ 2._____ 3._____ 4._____

GOAL ACTIVITIES

distinguishing between urgent and important tasks, reading selectively, delegating low priority tasks, and screening telephone calls.

You will probably have more ideas than time. Again, you will have to narrow down your choices to the ones essential to reaching your goals. Target two or three essential activities in Exercise 4.3 by circling the ones you wish to put into action.

❸ *Implement goal activities.* Finally, you must implement and evaluate your targeted activities. First, write a plan of implementation using Exercise 4.5. Begin by writing your activity (*what* you will be doing), then note *where* you will be doing it, *when* it will be done, *how often* you will do it, and *what* you expect to be the outcome. The key is to build the activity into your everyday work and life-style so you can progress naturally toward your goals. For example, if you wait for an unscheduled block of time in your office, say two hours, to begin writing a manuscript, you may never start, and consequently never end your writing project. You may have to make a commitment that every Tuesday morning you will retreat to your "high payoff hideout" and engage in your academic writing without telephone or drop-in visitor interruptions. Because you are accustomed to the confusion of the activity trap, you may be surprised by the silence.

This completes the last step in your professional and personal development and signals the beginning of its implementation. Professional development is a continuous process and should not be haphazardly planned or left to chance. You should specify a certain time each year to update and add new goals. Select a date of significance that can easily be remembered as your next goal session. The beginning of the semester or academic year is a perfect time. Go on a personal retreat and find time to reflect and dream. It will put your profession and life back in perspective.

As you can see, professional development is a process of defining, and redefining, your sights, always placing new and different size targets in front of you. Goal setting works in two directions: You work on them, and they work on you. The key is to change your habits into productive activities that reinforce your goals and aspirations. You may find you wished you picked more daisies...

> If you hold your nose to the grindstone rough,
> And hold it down there long enough,
> You'll soon forget there are such things
> As brooks that babble and birds that sing!
> These three things will your world compose,
> Just you, and a stone, and your darn old nose!
> If I had life to live over, I'd pick more daisies.
> (Author Unknown)

As you reflect on your academic career and personal life, what daisies do you still wish to pick?

Exercise 4.5
Implementing Your Plan

(1) Indicate below the *activities* you will use to fulfill your goal, *where* you will conduct them, *how often*, *when they will be completed*, and what outcomes you expect.

Goal Number	Activities	WHERE	HOW OFTEN	WHEN	Outcomes
	1.				
	2.				
	3.				
	4.				
	5.				
	6.				
	7.				
	8.				
	9.				
	10.				

References

Adams, J. D. (1980). *Understanding and managing stress.* San Diego, CA: University Associates.

Blackburn, R. T. (1979). Academic careers: Patterns and possibilities. In *Faculty career development* (Report No. 2). Washington, DC: ASHE-ERIC.

Bowen, H. R., & Schuster, J. H. (1986). *American professors: A national resource imperiled.* New York: Oxford University Press.

Caplan, R. D., Cobb, S., French, J. R. P., Van Harrison, R., & Pinneau, S. R. (1980). *Job demands and worker health: Main effects and occupational differences.* HEW Publication No. (N10SH), 75-160.

Dillard, C. (1992). *Leadership in a diverse society.* Administrative Internship Conference, Washington State University, Pullman, WA.

Fisher, W., & Ury, R. (1990). *Getting to yes: Negotiating agreement without giving in.* Boston: Houghton Mifflin.

Freeman, B. C. (1977). Faculty women in the American university: Up the down staircase. *Higher Education, 6,* 139-145.

Friedman, M., & Rosenman, R. (1974). *Type A behavior and your heart.* New York: Alfred A. Knopf.

Glasser, W. (1976). *Positive addiction.* New York: Harper & Row.

Gmelch, W. H. (1982). *Beyond stress to effective management.* New York: John Wiley & Sons.

Gmelch, W. H. (1983). Stress for success: How to optimize your performance. *Theory into Practice, 22(1),* 7-15.

Gmelch, W. H. (1987). What colleges and universities can do about faculty stress. In P. Seldin (Ed.), *Coping with Faculty Stress* (pp. 23-31). San Francisco: Jossey-Bass.

Gmelch, W. H. (1988). Educators' response to stress: Towards a coping taxonomy. *Journal of Educational Administration, 24(3),* 72-81.

Gmelch, W. H. (1991). Paying the price for academic leadership: Department chair trade-offs. *Educational Record, 72*(3), 45-49

Gmelch, W. H. (1992). The paradox of the swivel chair. *Universe Magazine, 5*(2), 10-11, 27.

Gmelch, W. H., Lovrich, N. P., & Wilke, P. K. (1984). Stress in academe: A national perspective. *Research in Higher Education, 20*(4), 477-490.

Gmelch, W. H., & Miskin, V. D. (1993). *Leadership skills for department chairs.* Boston: Anker.

Gmelch, W. H., & Wilke, P. K. (1991). The stresses of faculty and administrators in higher education. *Journal for Higher Education Management, 6*(2), 23-31.

Gmelch, W. H., Wilke, P. K., & Lovrich, N. P. (1986). Dimensions of stress among university faculty: Factor analytic results from a national study. *Research in Higher Education, 24*(3), 266-286.

Kanter, R. M. (1977). *Men and women of the corporation.* New York: Basic Books.

Keinan, G., & Perlberg, A. (1987). Stress in academe: A cross-cultural comparison between Israeli and American academicians. *Journal of Cross-Cultural Psychology, 18,* 193-207.

Kobasa, S. C., & Maddi, S. (1980). *The concepts of hardy executives.* Chicago: University of Chicago Press.

Koester, L. S., & Clark, C. H. (1980). *Academic job satisfaction: Differences related to sex and marital status.* Paper presented at the American Psychological Association, 88th Annual Convention.

Koontz, E. D. (1979). *A step toward equality: A progress report.* Washington, DC: National Manpower Institute.

Odiorne, G. S. (1974). *Management in the activity trap.* New York: Harper & Row.

Pelletier, K. R. (1977). *Mind as healer, mind as slayer.* New York: Dell.

Sargent, A. G. (1980). *The androgynous manager.* New York: AMACOM.

Selye, H. (1974). *Stress without distress.* Philadelphia: J.G. Lippincott.

Smith, E., & Jordan, M. (1993). Faculty stress and retention of junior black faculty at U.S. universities. *Research in Higher Education, 34*(2), 229-242.

Tack, M. W., & Patitu, C. L. (1992). *Faculty job satisfaction: Women and minorities in peril.* ASHE-ERIC Higher Education Report No. 4. Washington, DC: The George Washington University, School of Education and Human Development.

Tubesing, N. L., & Tubesing, D. A. (1982). The treatment of choice: Selecting stress skills to suit the individual and the situation. In W. S. Paine (Ed.), *Job stress and burnout: Research, theory and intervention perspectives* (pp. 155-171). Beverly Hills, CA: Sage.

Wilke, P. K., Gmelch, W. H., & Lovrich, N. P. (1985) Stress and productivity: Evidence of the inverted U-function. *Public Productivity Review, 9*(4), 342-356.

Additional Resources

Some faculty may be encouraged to read more in the area of stress and coping strategies. Researchers and writers have amassed an overwhelming body of knowledge about stress: more than 100,000 articles and books and 1,000 research projects. Although we often suffer from information overload, the following half dozen resources may assist you to understand more about the phenomenon of stress and to use it to your advantage.

Boice, R. (1992). *The new faculty member.* San Francisco: Jossey-Bass.

In this book, Robert Boice offers a range of strategies designed to help new faculty thrive. He identifies obstacles confronting new faculty members (gaining acceptance, establishing teaching styles and skills, and developing productive habits) and methods to overcome the obstacles (mentoring, teaching skills, and so on) as well as exploring the institutional support system.

Winfred, A. M., & de Guzman, R. M. (1983). *Burnout: The new academic disease* (Report No. 9). Washington, DC: ASHE-ERIC/Higher Education Research.

This monograph is one of dozens of ASHE-ERIC/Higher Education reports published on topics critical to higher education. This particular publication is based on surveys of almost 2,000 faculty members at 17 colleges and discusses burn-out in academe. The theoretical foundation is the person-environment fit model of stress from which the authors disclose factors within the person and factors in the work environment which cause stress. They conclude by reviewing the symptoms, examining roots, identifying stressors, and prescribing remedies for academic burnout.

Seldin, P. (1987). *Coping with faculty stress*. San Francisco: Jossey-Bass.

This volume in the Jossey-Bass *New Directions for Teaching and Learning* series spells out the specific causes of faculty stress and offers practical and proven ways of coping with the pressures facing professors. The nine chapters by contributing authors address the research findings about the causes of stress, actions that colleges can take to combat faculty stress, short-term coping techniques, long-term stress management, and faculty renewal programs.

Schuster, J., Wheeler, D. W., & Associates (1990). *Enhancing faculty careers: Strategies for development and renewal*. San Francisco: Jossey-Bass.

Because one of the major faculty stressors is "career progress not what it should be," this book is particularly well suited for faculty seeking to enhance their careers. The leading authorities in the field provide strategies, programs, and supports to develop faculty members professionally and personally. The authors describe faculty development programs for wellness, career consulting, graduate school preparation, employee assistance, and retirement in addition to an array of other programs and models that can be adapted on any campus.

Also, other books in Sage's *Survival Skills for Scholars Series* in which this monograph appears, teach faculty members basic professional skills to help ameliorate the stresses of daily life in the university. Among the more relevant books in the series are the following volumes:

Getting Tenure, by Marcia Lynn Whicker, Jennie Jacobs Kronenfeld, & Ruth Ann Strickland.
Effective Committee Service, by Neil J. Smelser
Confronting Diversity Issues on Campus, by Benjamin P. Bowser, Gale S. Auletta, & Terry Jones
Improving Your Classroom Teaching, Maryellen Weimer

The top journals in higher education also provide the most recent research and critical thinking regarding faculty issues related to stress.

You may wish to consult the following journals:

Innovative Higher Education
The Journal of Higher Education
Research in Higher Education
Review of Higher Education

The higher education professional associations such as the Association of the Study of Higher Education (ASHE), American Educational Research Association (AERA Division J), POD, and the American Association of Higher Education (AAHE) also provide information and support for the development faculty.

About the Author

Walter H. Gmelch is a professor and chair of the Educational Administration Department at Washington State University where he also serves as Director of the UCEA Center for the Study of Department Chair. An educator, management consultant, university administrator, and former business executive, Dr. Gmelch has conducted research and written extensively on the topics of leadership, team development, conflict, stress, and time management, and has published more than 50 articles and a dozen books on management, co-authoring a book entitled *Strategic Leadership Skills for Department Chairs.*

In addition he has presented more than 400 workshops throughout the United States, Asia, Europe, Africa, and Australia to universities, colleges, schools, public agencies, and corporations. Dr. Gmelch has received numerous honors including a Kellogg Fellowship, Danforth Leadership Program, Excellence in Research Award, Australian Research Fellow, University Council for Educational Administration Distinguished Professor Award, and Education Press Award of America. He earned a Ph.D. in the Educational Executive Program from the University of California at Santa Barbara, an M.B.A. from the University of California at Berkeley, a B.A. from Stanford University, and an A.A. from the College of San Mateo.